REMEMBERING
Lee County

REMEMBERING
Lee County
Where Winter Spends the Summer

Prudy Taylor Board

Charleston   London

History
PRESS

Published by The History Press
Charleston, SC 29403
www.historypress.net

The cover image of the lovely lass picking oranges in a Lee County citrus grove was taken in the late 1940s and used in Chamber of Commerce brochures. *Courtesy of the Southwest Florida Historical Museum.*

First published 2006

Manufactured in the United Kingdom

ISBN-10 1.59629.102.8
ISBN-13 978.1.59629.102.7

Library of Congress Cataloging-in-Publication Data

Board, Prudy Taylor
  Remembering Lee County, Florida : where winter spends the summer / Prudy Taylor Board.
      p. cm.
  Includes bibliographical references.
  ISBN-13: 978-1-59629-102-7 (alk. paper)
  ISBN-10: 1-59629-102-8 (alk. paper)
  1. Lee County (Fla.)--History. 2. Lee County (Fla.)--History--Anecdotes.
3. Lee County (Fla.)--History, Local. 4. Lee County (Fla.)--Biography. I. Title.
  F317.L3B643 2006
  975.9'48--dc22
                    2006027584

Contents

Contents

PREFACE

For years, the ears on the *Fort Myers News-Press* read, "Where Winter Spends the Summer," and I always thought that was very appropriate. My folks had returned to our home in Pennsylvania shortly after I was born and didn't return to Florida for years. Growing up in Pennsylvania, I remember well slogging through snow on my way to school, icy sidewalks strewn with ashes from the furnace to keep them from being slippery, and snowshoes and galoshes and heavy snowsuits, and colds and pneumonia— well, you get the picture. When we returned to Lee County, I was thrilled— and I realized early on that the ears on the newspaper told the truth: Lee County really is where winter spends the summer. But Lee County when I grew up here was so much more than climate; it was filled to overflowing with caring, generous, supportive, quirky people who played important roles in my adolescence. As a result, this book, while ostensibly a collection of columns I've written over the years, is also a bit of a love note to my hometown and the county in which it resides. (One last thought: this book is a companion to *Remembering Fort Myers: The City of Palms*, and yet you'll find historical information about Fort Myers in this book as well. I've been careful not to repeat any material, but it would be impossible to omit Fort Myers since it is the county seat and, more than that, was the center of government, business and social life for more than a century.)

ACKNOWLEDGEMENTS

Over the years I've been fortunate to work with some great men and women, beginning with Joe Workman and Jo Daughtrey Bigelow, my editors at the *News-Press*. I can't omit Don Godfrey, who launched the original *Lee Living* in 1978 and had enough confidence in me to name me managing editor (when I asked him what a managing editor does, he said, "A managing editor manages and you can do that."); Vince Smith, golf writer, friend and good guy extraordinaire who brought me on as managing editor of *Home & Condo*; Bev and Inez Bevelacqua, publishers of *Home & Condo*; Jack McCarthy, who published the renaissance of *Lee Living*; and also another great guy I've been fortunate to count as a friend, Don Bottorff, who for years was the executive director of the Fort Myers Chamber of Commerce. These people gave me a chance to grow as a writer and to learn even more about my home. And, of course, I can never thank the staff at the Southwest Florida Historical Museum enough—Matt, Victor, Carol, Sara—you're great. And finally, thanks to two of my favorite women: Maureen Bashaw, who put up with my noisy interruptions into her life and home, and to local historian Kathryn Wilbur, who was so generous with her time and help and friendship.

PLUCKY PIONEERS
Newspapers Take Root in Southwest Florida
1884–1916

The year was 1884. The 139.43 acres that composed the original site of the town of Fort Myers had been platted and the plat recorded in the Monroe County seat at Key West a scant eight years earlier.

However, the town that had now grown to about fifty families did not have a newspaper. So when the opportunity to "kidnap" an editor and his printing press presented itself, Henry L. Roan, captain of the schooner *Lily White*, wasted no time.

Stafford C. Cleveland, publisher of the *Yates County Chronicle* in Penn Yan, New York, had decided to come to Florida because of poor health. He was headed for Fort Ogden. At the terminus of the railroad in Cedar Key, he boarded the *Lily White*.

As Karl Grismer writes in *The Story of Fort Myers*, "Captain Roan knew as well as anyone that Fort Myers needed a newspaper and when he learned he had a bona fide newspaper editor on board, and a whole newspaper plant to boot, he made up his mind that editor Cleveland would never get to Fort Ogden—not if he could help it. So instead of going into Charlotte Harbor and stopping first at Fort Ogden as he ordinarily did, Captain Roan headed straight for Fort Myers."

When he docked, Captain Roan hurried uptown and gathered together a band of local businessmen who convinced Cleveland that he should set

Stafford C. Cleveland, editor and publisher of Fort Myers's first newspaper. *Courtesy of the Southwest Florida Historical Museum.*

up his business here. The first issue of the *Fort Myers Press* was published November 22, 1884.

Unfortunately, Cleveland's stint as publisher was not to last; he died on December 3, 1885. His widow carried on, publishing the *Press* until March 13, 1886, when Frank Stout bought the paper, coming from *The Recorder* in Holton, Kansas, and *The Agriculturist* in Deland.

The details of Stout's background were published in May of that same year. Making front-page news along with him was a Plant City farmer who had received eight dollars for his first barrel of Irish potatoes shipped north. Under state news, it was also reported that "Palatka has lady barbers," and that a Jacksonville policeman had been fired for getting drunk.

By 1890, Stout and the *Press* were both fixtures in the community. In the January 2 edition, he published a poem by a local poet with the initials J.C.J. Titled "Fort Myers," the first stanza was a presage of years to come:

> *Fort Myers, you're looking all your best;*
> *You're making rapid strides,*
> *You're growing east, you're growing west*
> *You're growing on all sides.*

The same issue carried an item that read "Somebody was seen to get a marriage license New Year's Day and we may report a wedding in our next issue," along with the news that the body of a drowned man had been found floating on Lostman's Key by hunters from Chokoloskee. It also carried a report that Thomas J. Evans had brought a radish "that was 18 inches in length, 10 inches in circumference and weight 3½ pounds to the *Press* office."

Stout had no competition until 1894, when the first *Tropical News* was formed and edited by Philip Isaacs. Apparently, there wasn't room for two newspapers in the small community. An editorial in August 1895 read "Good bye! We have sold the *Press*, building and lot to Chas. W. Hill, late of Jerauld County, S.D."

Hill wrote, "In assuming the responsibility of editor of a public journal, it is but a reasonable expectation of the people who are expected to be its patrons and readers, to look for an introductory outlining the object and course to be pursued by its editor."

In outlining its course, he notes "the expectation of having a following of quite a number of our relatives and friends from the northwestern states as soon as they learn…that the months of June, July, August and September, in Lee County, Fla., are not dangerous to the health of the people."

Hill lasted one summer, but it wasn't his health that deterred him. By November, he wrote, "Owing to the hard and close times from whence I came, at the north, I find it impossible to meet my payments."

And Stout, in once again assuming the responsibility for the paper, added, "As will be seen by the above, there's many a slip between the lip and the dipper."

That was his bad news. The good news he reported was that "I have associated with me in the business, my son, Nathan G. Stout. We will be able to run the *Press* until Hades freezes over and then run it on the congelement [*sic*], unless sooner sold to some good, live Democrat and man of ability."

Hades apparently froze the following March, for that month Stout wrote, "It is with unfeigned gratification that we resign the *Press* to such worthy and upright men as J.D. Rose and Hal B. Selby."

In a stringer's column, "Buckingham Briefs," it was reported in the same paper that "the citizens of this community met at the schoolhouse Tuesday evening, and organized a literary society." The column further reported that a picnic at Clay's Bridge had been a pleasant affair, but "the croquet game was spoiled through the intervention of two young men who had failed to secure partners." It seems the two young men had been sent ahead to clean away the debris in preparation for the game, but instead they "borrowed" the croquet set and found as partners two girls who had not gone to the picnic.

In January 1897, Rose and Selby were still there and had consolidated the *Fort Myers Press*, "the official paper of the Town of Fort Myers," with the *Tropical News* and the following March, Selby sold his interest to Rose and retired from newspaper work.

The game of editorial musical chairs continued. In May of 1897, Rose announced he was selling his interest in the paper to Nathan G. Stout, "a young man, full of life and vigor." In the same paper, W.G. Mendenhall advertised "mattresses made to order, either moss, hair, excelsior or cotton."

Christmas was celebrated with vigor in those early years. In the December 28, 1889 issue, it was reported that "the biggest attraction on Christmas Day was the tournament held on First Street. There were nine riders." The story continued, "The most startling thing that happened…was an accident to Frank Carson's horse…Frank has had to go off and hide to keep from answering the everlasting string of questions…We feel for him and therefore make it known to one and all that the horse broke his leg and Frank is doing as well as could be expected under the circumstances."

But where was the spirit of publish or perish? The editorial that same day read "The *Press* makes no pretense to getting out much of a local paper this week, on account of the Christmas holiday and also for the reason that we have been breaking down our old press and putting up our cylinder press in its place. We hope by next week to have everything in working order and to have all the local happenings."

Three items down was a short article that read "My son has been troubled for years with chronic diarrhea." Thomas G. Bower of Glencoe, Ohio, wrote that he had convinced his son to take some of Chamberlain's Colic, Cholera and Diarrhea Remedy. After using two bottles, he'd been cured.

In the meantime, the situation had stabilized at the *Fort Myers Press*. Philip Isaacs, who'd come on board from the *Tropical News*, and Nathan G. Stout had settled into a relationship that was to last for years.

By 1902, 209 students were enrolled in county schools. In an editorial about truancy, Isaacs wrote, "There is very little sickness in the community, and we wonder why the average attendance is 85 percent and isn't nearer 100 percent."

That same year, trouble brewed in Arcadia. A story headlined "DeSoto County Grand Jury In Action" reported, "Some of the best-known citizens of DeSoto County have been indicted by the grand jury for cow stealing." The article revealed that twenty-five persons, among them a former tax collector, had been charged. The following week, the *Press* reported that a Stockman's Protective Association had been formed in Arcadia. Each of the cattlemen had sworn not to assist anyone charged with the crime of cow stealing.

Tarpon fishing was one of Lee County's main claims to fame beginning in the 1880s. This fisherman was posing with his catch on Useppa Island. *Courtesy of the Southwest Florida Historical Museum.*

For years, the *Press* had carried only occasional information about other communities, but the February 5, 1903 edition reported "Punta Gorda's Marshal Murdered." The story explained that "J.H. Bowman, marshal of the town of Punta Gorda, was shot and killed while sitting in his home…The fatal load was from a shotgun, nine buckshot taking effect behind the right ear, killing him instantly…The crime is one of the most dastardly ever committed in this section of the state, and every effort is being made to apprehend the assassin." No one had been seen and the clues were sparse; the *Press* later accurately predicted "the culprit may never be apprehended."

The winter of 1904 was a good one for the citrus crop. The *Press* reported "Most Records Broken For Orange Shipments. A Special Train of Eleven Cars Going Out Tuesday…Mr. Booth's books show that 5,501 boxes of oranges and 1,780 boxes of grapefruit have been shipped out the past week…The special orange train now leaves here at 7 p.m. on every other night…On Sunday, a special train of eight cars, containing 2,382 boxes left here at 5 p.m.….arriving in Lakeland at 9:10 p.m.…. arriving faster than the regular passenger schedule."

Pineapple was also an important crop here. The paper reported "Capt. R.B. Storter came up Monday with his auxiliary schooner, *Bertie Lee*, with the first load of pineapples from U.S. Marshal John F. Horr's plantation on Horr's Island."

Tarpon fishing was much in vogue. This area jealously guarded its reputation as the finest spot for the sport. "Greedy East Coast," complained article headlines in June of 1905, "Now Lays Claim to All the Tarpon Record. Figures on Which They Base Their Claims Will Make Old Tarpon Fishers Laugh." And that was just the headline. "Again the greedy folks over the East Coast are laying claim to all that is on the earth, in the heavens above and in the waters underneath," the story read. And in the same issue, it was reported that "Lord Falconer of England, who has been fishing at Boca Grande two weeks this month, has killed 30 tarpon. Mr. Mygatt had landed 20 tarpon at Boca Grande in one day."

One of the biggest news stories of 1905 was the destruction of Arcadia's business district by fire. In a special supplement to the *Fort Myers Press* that December, it was reported, "Fire, which originated in an outbuilding owned by Gore & Scott, at 12:30 this morning, and which raged uninterrupted for hours, wiped out practically the entire business portion of the town, sweeping all that portion west of the railroad tracks."

News from that issue of the *Press* continued with an item from Estero. "John E. Hall got back from the fair last Friday. John was pretty well used up, but says he had a good time."

By 1910, the railroad had come to Fort Myers and southwest Florida. The Atlantic Coast Line was advertising its dining car and trains with romantic names: Dixie Flyer and Seminole Limited.

And Dr. Franklin Miles, who had established Miles Laboratories in Elkhart, Indiana, and developed Nervine and Alka Seltzer, had bought a winter home in Fort Myers. He invited a writer for the *Press* to visit his "down river home."

"The trip," wrote the reporter, "was a most delightful one on the launch *Chipmunk*, owned by Dr. Miles...The thing that drew our attention was an artesian well that has a capacity of 47,000 gallons of water per hour."

The tour of Dr. Miles's home was noteworthy because he was experimenting with new crops that might be grown here and indeed, the reporter observed that "bananas, tropical fruits and orange groves were growing.

"Leaving this part of the farm, we were conducted to the part known as The Jungle, which extends out to what is commonly known as Nigger Head. We went through the jungle and came out to the pride of the farm, a 27-acre Irish potato field...The prospects are rosy for a fine yield."

March 9, 1910, was designated Fort Myers Day to commemorate the twenty-fifth year of incorporation. "Capt. F.A. Hendry, that grand old pioneer," was to speak. The celebration included a "Historical Pageant

Embracing Twenty-five Years of Progress. The procession will be led by Indians and cowboys and ox-carts as seen 20 years ago. The school children will be in the line of march with their banners."

A *Press* reporter made the front page on December 16, 1912—by getting shot. Maud Nichols had been shot by a recent candidate for mayor, Percy Jones. It seems that Miss Nichols had been "trying to protect her sister, who was married to Jones of Fort Myers."

While not sparing Jones, the editorial expressed relief that Miss Nichols would recover and hoped "for her safety and guidance after she shall have been restored to health again. May she and all other unprotected young women have the gift of reasoning that keeps them in the path of safety. God help our girls and young women to be wary of the results of attempting to reform men single-handed."

Jones, the paper reported, "comes from an old and well-known family of this city [Tampa] and but for the demon drink…might have had a bright career."

By 1913, Nathan G. Stout had wearied of the newspaper business and had moved on, selling the *Press* to T.M. Callahan. At this time, the paper reported, "To date but one mile remains to be graded on the work of construction of the new McGregor Boulevard running from this city to Punta Rassa."

The following year was marked by one of the most disastrous blazes in Fort Myers's history when the Lee County Packing House, the "largest building in the world devoted exclusively to the packing of citrus fruits, was entirely consumed by fire last night with all its contents; also the Lofton machine shops…the steamer *Thomas A. Edison* and nearly a dozen small yachts and pleasure boats."

The people working near the fire were blistered, the paper reported. The Towles warehouse caught fire, the flames had been doused, but gasoline tanks on the Ireland dock containing nearly 15,000 gallons were in danger. The fire, the paper pointed out, showed "how badly Fort Myers needs fire protection" and led to the purchase of an expensive, up-to-date fire engine, the area's first. Then, in August 1914, World War I broke out and although the United States would not enter the war until April 1917, it was very much on everyone's mind. And when the United States did go to war, Lee County sent its share of young men.

Originally published in the *Fort Myers News-Press* on November 7, 1984.

SOUTHWEST FLORIDA MARCHED FORWARD IN WAR AND PEACE

1917–1949

Patriotic spirit ran high. As 1917 ended, the *Fort Myers Press* was listing the names of local men called to military duty on the front page. If a man didn't qualify or didn't show up to register, that was front-page news as well. A chicken dinner for forty cents was advertised by the Leon Hotel on December 31. In the same edition, the *Press* alerted readers, "In accordance with the custom which has been followed by the *Press*, there will be no issue of this paper tomorrow, the force taking advantage of that opportunity to enjoy a holiday."

But January 1 wasn't a holiday for everyone. The ladies of the Red Cross, upon learning they were short six hundred abdominal bandages to be sent to the soldiers overseas, "vowed to work New Year's Day." World War I continued in the forefront of the news through most of 1918. Bread was rationed to two ounces per meal in hotels, restaurants and dining cars. Mondays and Wednesdays were wheatless days. Tuesdays were meatless and Saturdays were porkless.

The times weren't completely joyless. On February 20, girls from throughout Lee County—which included what are now Collier and Hendry Counties—vied for the honor of portraying Princess Florida in the Great Indian Pageant.

The *Fort Myers Press* cost three cents. It was managed by Tom Callahan, nephew of John T. Murphy, who, according to Karl Grismer in *The Story of*

Lee County men stepped forward to do their duty in World War I. In this photo, Lieutenant Guy Strayhorn inspected the troops as they prepared to ship out from the local train station. *Courtesy of Bruce Strayhorn.*

Fort Myers, was a newspaper publisher from Superior, Wisconsin, who had wintered here. Murphy had purchased the paper for $8,000 in 1914.

Grismer wrote that Murphy had tried repeatedly to induce the managing editor of the *Superior Evening Telegram* to take charge of the paper here, but Carl Hanton wasn't interested. Armistice was declared on November 11, 1918, and, as the war came to a close, Lee County settled down to enjoy a period of peaceful prosperity almost unparalleled in America's history. Real estate values soared and southwest Florida drew people from all around the country.

The year 1920 was significant both for the *Fort Myers Press* and for women. In February, the *Press* reported that "the *Fort Myers Tropical News*, a new newspaper that will be issued twice a week by the Bentz Publishing Company, made its first appearance here Wednesday." *The Press* welcomed the *Tropical News* into the "journalistic field," but also expressed doubt that the community would be able to support two papers.

The *Tropical News* was to be published Tuesdays and Thursdays and cost three dollars yearly. *The Press*, which had been a daily since 1911, cost seven dollars a year, but also published a weekly on Thursdays, which cost two dollars yearly.

In September of that year, the voter registration books of Florida were opened to women. In Lee County, Minnie A. Stone, wife of a local doctor, was the first woman to register.

To the south, Marco Island was making news as "the site of the greatest canning industries in the south." The *Press* reported that "over 700 bushels of clams in cans and in glass jars are put up in Marco and the vicinity every working day." The factories, which had been founded nine years earlier by J.H. Doxsee and Sons, owed a great deal to Captain W.D. Collier, the *Press* wrote. He had not only founded the community in 1872, he had also discovered the first clam beds and had devised dredges specifically geared for digging clams. (He was of no relation to the family after which Collier County would be named.)

In 1923, the issue of dividing Lee County into Lee, Collier and Hendry Counties drew controversy. Spearheaded by Barron G. Collier, who was anxious to develop his interests in south Lee County, the issue came to a vote in Tallahassee that May. The legislation passed and Hendry and Collier Counties came into being July 9.

But it had been a tough and vicious battle. The *Press* had expressed no opposition to the formation of Hendry County. Indeed, the editorial of May 2, 1923, read "The creation of Hendry County, the one and only issue in the June primary, was voted upon favorably by the people." However, the editorial continued, "this morning an airplane piloted by W.C. Bunn with Maxwell M. Brennan, overseas veteran, as a passenger, left Fort Myers for Tallahassee with the petitions bearing the names of 804 qualified voters calling upon Rep. R.A. Henderson to resign because by fostering Collier County, he does not represent the wishes of his constituents."

A whimsical note appeared in the next day's edition. "An Alva citizen… was busy this morning circulating an eleventh-hour petition at Buckingham favoring the creation of Collier County on the premise…that Rep. Henderson will favor the further creation of Ford County with Alva as the county seat."

Despite the controversy, Lee County and its neighboring counties continued to grow. From a population of 9,540 in 1920, Lee County had grown to 14,990 by 1930—even in the face of the fact that it had been split into three counties. (Growth would be slowed by the Great Depression. By 1940, the population had only risen to 17,488.)

The *Fort Myers Press* changed hands again in 1924. Grismer writes, "A controlling interest in the paper was purchased by Harrison Fuller who had resigned a position as assistant managing editor of the St. Paul *Pioneer Press* to form a publicity agency in partnership with Carl Hanton, who was then working for the *Pioneer Press*. The purchase price was $35,000. Hanton finally came to the area as managing editor of the *Press* in 1925 and three years later when Fuller went to New York, Hanton took over control of the paper [the *Fort Myers Press*]."

In 1928, the Tamiami Trail was completed at a cost of $9 million. Earlier, in 1914, south Floridians had dreamed of the day when Tampa, Fort Myers, Naples and Miami would be connected by a road passable in both wet and dry seasons, but insufficient funding and arguments over the best route slowed progress. Then the United States entered World War I—and the trail was temporarily forgotten. After the war ended, work resumed.

Also in 1928, a new bridge was built over Matanzas Pass connecting Fort Myers Beach with the mainland. It replaced a wooden span that had washed out in the September 1926 hurricane.

By January 1929, the *Fort Myers Press* reported that Barron Collier had enlarged and improved the Hotel Charlotte Harbor in Punta Gorda and announced the upcoming visit of President and Mrs. Calvin Coolidge. The Palm Lodge on Sanibel was advertising rates of five dollars a day, thirty dollars a week and twenty-eight dollars weekly by the month. The Franklin Arms Hotel was promoting a businessman's lunch at seventy-five cents and dinner at one dollar.

One highlight of 1929 was Thomas Edison's birthday celebration, which drew Henry Ford, Harvey Firestone and President-elect Herbert Hoover to Fort Myers.

"Small Army of News Cameramen Record Event For Nation At Large" read a headline, and "School Children Visited by Distinguished Quartet of Americans Who Motor Through Flag Lined Streets To Music Of Drum Corps and Band."

Early in 1929 articles about the instability of the stock market had begun to appear. By July, a headline in the *Tropical News* read "U.S. Rushes Millions To Aid Florida Banks." The article detailed the transfer of $5 million from the Federal Reserve Bank in Atlanta to a Tampa bank.

A run on banks was also feared locally. In July the *Tropical News* reported, "Bank of Fort Myers Stocks Up With Cash To Ward Off Flurry…Counters to be stacked high with money to pay depositors if demanded." Bank President J.E. Foxworthy was quoted as saying, "There will be plenty of money to pay off every depositor who cares to withdraw." Although a crisis was averted, many southwest Floridians would lose their savings in local banks in the years that followed.

In November, the *Tropical News* reported its own story on the front page, headlined "Justice of Peace Charges Contempt by *Tropical News*." The charges stemmed from a news story about traffic cases in a court in which two African Americans were tried. "One of them," a reporter wrote, "was fined $1 and $14 [in court costs] for driving a truck without a license tag which he said he had lost which he later produced."

Summoned to appear in court on charges of "belittling, embarrassing and impairing the efficiency" of the court were managing editor Carl Hanton and city editor Bill Spear. The same issue also carried an Associated Press story from Washington, D.C., headlined "3 Reporters Jailed For Contempt Gain Freedom on Bonds."

A few days later, the *Tropical News* included another name known and respected in the area, Circuit Judge George W. Whitehurst, the man for whom the federal building in downtown Fort Myers is named. Whitehurst exonerated the *Tropical News* in the contempt case.

The editorial of the day read "Three Washington reporters were sent to jail for contempt because they didn't tell something the court wanted to know. Another way [to go to jail] is to tell something the court doesn't want known."

In the 1930s, the Depression became the major concern of the area's two newspapers and its readers. The *Tropical News* and the *Fort Myers Press* merged in June of 1931, becoming the *Fort Myers News-Press*. At first an afternoon paper, it was changed to a morning paper after its readers were polled. Spear left early in 1931 to work at the *Boston Herald* and returned to the *News-Press* in 1947 after a number of years with the Associated Press and *Stars and Stripes* during World War II.

Throughout the 1930s, tourism remained big business and big news in the area. "Chamber reports 51 new visitors," read one story. Next to that was a report that the Loyal Bible Class of the First Christian Church had enjoyed an auto party at a member's home.

"The house was decorated with tires and automobile accessories," the society reporter wrote. "Games were played including 'assembling the car,' 'filling the radiator,' and 'changing a tire' after which the party retired to a 'filling station' where refreshments of doughnuts and coffee were served."

As the decade drew to a close, economic recovery was in the wind. The *News-Press* noted that "Santa Claus filled up Fort Myers' stockings this year. Most of the stores never did such a business and those that could find the equal of this year had to go back to the 1925 boom.

"No doubt," the editorial continued, "the per capita wealth is much less than we figured in those halcyon days but at any rate, most people had enough this year to see them through their Christmas shopping and make it a prosperous one for the stores as well as a merry one for themselves."

Ronald Halgrim was city editor when the nation plunged into World War II after the Japanese attack on Pearl Harbor on December 7, 1941. Again the front pages of the *News-Press* were filled with news of the war.

And again the residents of southwest Florida cut back and accepted without complaint the dictates of the Office of Price Administration.

Tokens and ration stamps became as important, and in some instances more important, as currency.

Within two years, shoes cost $1.99 plus some ration coupons. Butter was almost impossible to buy. A 1942 Pontiac was selling for $1,356. People were listening to H.V. Kaltenborn and Lowell Thomas on their radios along with shows featuring Chinese detective Charlie Chan, cowboy hero Tom Mix and the Lone Ranger.

The Royal Palm Flying Service at Page Field advertised lessons with solo courses as low as sixty-four dollars. It cost thirty-five dollars to fly round-trip to Tampa. In southwest Florida, women were working—to judge by the want ads—as waitresses and sales ladies.

Again, the *News-Press* reported on its men at war, along with lists of casualties, on the front page. Those figures mounted, but the war finally ended.

"WAR OVER," screamed the *News-Press* headlines on August 14, 1945. "Fort Myers celebrated the surrender of Japan with a burst of rejoicing last night which began soon after the official announcement at Washington at 7 p.m., and continued far into the night," the paper revealed.

Of the nighttime festivities, the *News-Press* reported,

> *There was a constant stream of cars going in both directions with horns at full blast. Trucks picked up loads of youngsters who sang and shouted. Some clanged cowbells, others tied tin cans to the rear bumpers. A few persons found some hoarded giant fire crackers and had fun tossing them toward the curb.*
>
> *The liquor stores closed promptly at 7 o'clock on the surrender announcement….Numbers of persons made belated dashes to the package stores but they were out of luck. But there was open drinking on the streets as those who had looked ahead shared their bottles with thirsty brethren.*

The celebrations were so strenuous that "an informal parade announced by some enthusiasts early in the evening to take place at 11 p.m. was called off when the celebrants proved too tired to walk after four hours of whoopee."

That was the unofficial celebration. Officially, Mayor Dave Shapard issued an order that all cars must be off streets in the downtown parade route by 10:00 a.m. All the stores closed that August 15. Chairman Jack Holst of the American Legion Victory committee invited every patriotic, civic and fraternal group to participate in the parade, which was headed by a car carrying Mayor Shapard; County Commission Chairman Harry Stringfellow; Colonel James S. Sutton, commander of the Aerial Gunnery School at Buckingham; and Colonel James S. Coward, Page Field commander.

World War II had a lasting impact on southwest Florida. Before, visitors had been mainly wealthy people who wintered here. Now the servicemen who had trained at Buckingham and Page Field were to return to this area not merely to visit, but to live, work and raise their families. These men would make many and significant contributions to Lee County.

Originally published in the *Fort Myers News-Press* on November 14, 1984.

THE BOOM THAT DIDN'T GO BUST

1950–1984

L ee County sailed into the second half of the twentieth century. The sky was clear, the temperature was seventy-seven degrees that New Year's Day and all was right with southwest Florida and its world. Carl Hanton was president of the *News-Press*, William R. Spear was editor and Chesley F. Perry was general manager. Robert "Pep" Pepper was news editor. Dewey Murphy was advertising director and Tom Mathieson was circulation manager.

"WELCOME 1950!" enthused the New Year's Day editorial and as the new decade unrolled, Lee County boasted a population of 23,404, an increase from the U.S. Census of 1940, when the population was 17,488.

But Fort Myers was still a small river town where the birth of the first baby of the year stirred local merchants into giving free gifts: a baby blanket and down payment on a washing machine from Reaves Appliances. Frizzell Hardware offered a free bassinette to both the first girl and the first baby boy born.

A front-page story by Tom Morgan remarked that "Fort Myers passed a new milestone in its development during 1949 as city building permits neared the $2 million mark and probably established an all-time high."

Fort Myers was planning to celebrate its one-hundred-year-old origins as an army fort with a $5,000 tarpon-fishing tournament. On the education

Shrimpboats such as these at the Columbia Docks became a common sight in the 1950s. *Photo from the author's collection.*

beat, the construction of a new $700,000 Fort Myers Junior-Senior High School on Cortez Boulevard was underway.

Drugs were not a problem, but that "Ole Debbil [*sic*] Sex" had reared its head, as witnessed by a letter from a "Disgusted Teen" that ran in a Dear Abby column.

"I have just come from the newsstand," the letter read. "Have you seen what is put out for us to read? 'I LEARNED ABOUT SIN FROM MY HIGH SCHOOL TEACHER,' and 'WE WENT STEADY ONE NIGHT TOO LONG.' Also, 'I WAS CHASED BY A LOVE-WILD GIRL,' and 'I'M GOING TO MARRY THE FIRST MAN I SEE.'" Dear Abby's response was to the point: "Don't blame the people who publish them. They don't care if it smells as long as it ell."

The 1950s saw Lee County's population almost double, going from 23,404 to 45,600. A new industry was born when a shrimper from St. Augustine discovered beds of pink shrimp in the Dry Tortugas. Boats from St. Augustine, Fernandina and North and South Carolina hurried here to harvest the "pink gold," as the shrimp were quickly tagged.

An editorial in May of 1953 pointed to the bright side of a disaster. When fire destroyed the packinghouse of the Lee County Packing Co. on the riverfront, the good news was that this "cleared the way for opening up Edwards Drive through to Citrus Street, now the southbound Tamiami Trail, and for the construction of the downtown municipal parking lot."

And in 1954, the Corkscrew Swamp Bird and Wildlife Sanctuary was established through the efforts of the National Audubon Society.

Another boost to the local economy came in 1957 when a special act in the Florida legislature provided for the establishment here of a new state institution for the mentally retarded. Lee County donated the land, the state paid $5.5 million to construct Sunland Training Center and new jobs were opened for area residents.

Of paramount importance was the development of both Cape Coral and Lehigh Acres during the 1950s. Although old-timers had sneered when the developers began their marketing campaigns, and complained about the "overly enthusiastic" sales methods of Gulf American, both communities flourished.

In 1959, an editorial writer for the *News-Press* concluded, "The 1950s were good to Fort Myers and Lee County and we should be sorry to see them end tonight—except that the 1960s promise to be even better."

As southwest Florida moved into the '60s, everything did look bright. "Construction Hits $7 Million Mark as Boom Continues," reported *News-Press* staff writer Jewell Dean on January 1, 1960. George Sanders had taken out a $750,000 permit to build the Boulevard Plaza and George Moody secured permits for one hundred homes to be built in Tropic Isles in North Fort Myers.

Reporter Pete Packett (he was to become city editor by the end of the decade) collected a mélange of predictions that came incredibly close to what would happen in the 1980s. "The sun rises today on a brand new decade expected to be filled with progress and problems," Packett wrote. He quoted Mayor Gerald M. French as saying, "Man, it's going to be fantastic! You won't know this place."

It was predicted that Lee County's population would skyrocket to 100,000, which led a *News-Press* editorial writer (probably editor Bill Spears, it sounds like him!) to comment, "If Lee County is to have 100,000 people by 1960, let's hope they all drive small cars."

Florida Power & Light officials confidently estimated they'd have approximately 50,000 customers in the Fort Myers area. Inter-County Telephone & Telegraph spokesmen reported they had 17,993 customers and predicted they'd have 51,588 by 1970.

Lee County School Superintendent Ray Tipton predicted there would be 25,000 students in school by 1970 and tax assessor W. Stanley Hanson said the county's property tax base might even approach $350 million by 1970 if conditions continued.

Real estate ads revealed that one could buy thirty acres on Sanibel with some Gulf frontage, also road frontage, for $1,750 an acre. If that was too much for your pocketbook, you could look at one hundred acres on County Road south of town near the Tamiami Trail that was selling for $300 an acre. And for less than $18,000 you could have bought a two-bedroom, two-bath home right on McGregor Boulevard just past the Edison Home. The house included an upstairs apartment, which was renting for $85 a month on a yearly lease.

However, not all was growth. Fort Myers had been a cow town since before the Civil War, but now the cattle population had declined by seven thousand head in just a few short years. Higher land costs and the "advance of subdivision developers" were cited as reasons for the decrease.

At the same time, the vegetable-growing industry was hurting as a result of the frozen foods technology. Where once local growers could depend on the market for fresh vegetables, now the convenience of frozen vegetables made them available at a lower cost and on a year-round basis. Sweet corn was no longer a major local crop and the number of acres planted in Irish potatoes had diminished as well.

In the early 1960s, the flower-growing business was a relatively young industry. Gladioli and chrysanthemums were the most plentifully grown, but they were considered luxury items and their sales would depend on the national economy. More hope was placed on the budding business of ornamental nurseries.

"The development of so many subdivisions and the construction of hundreds of new homes should boom the business of ornamental nurseries whose products are used for landscaping," a *News-Press* writer opined.

The decade of the 1960s was indeed to see Lee County's population rise from 45,000 to 105,216, which led a *News-Press* correspondent to write in her column titled "North Fort Myers Highlights," "Coming back for a firsthand inspection of home territory is Mrs. Guy B. Smith, now of Tampa, and Mrs. Ruby Credle of Jacksonville…It seems they are having difficulty finding any old landmarks."

It was easy to understand why. Even the *News-Press* had moved from its location in the Collier Arcade after thirty-one years in the same spot. Diners at the Snack House had not eaten to the rhythm and clanking of the presses since 1961, when the press and delivery departments had been moved to the location on Anderson Avenue, but by May 1965 the relocation had been completed when the news and advertising departments moved to the same site.

In a story in the May 30, 1965 edition of the *News-Press*, it was reported that a new sixty-four-page press rolled for the first time.

The sixty-four-page Goss press doubled the paper's capacity. Yet an article reported, "the *News-Press* Thursday issue was 60 pages, and before much longer the press capacity will be increased again."

Fort Myers and Lee County reflected the social upheaval of the nation as a whole. In 1963 the segregation signs at the courthouse were taken down. Schools were desegregated in the mid-'60s. There were a number of racial incidents at Lee County campuses, but the few injuries were minor. It was also in the 1960s that Edison Junior College was built and opened for classes.

Signs of remarkable progress in southwest Florida were everywhere. It was in the '60s that the Caloosahatchee Bridge, the Cape Coral Bridge, the Sanibel Causeway, the Bonita Beach Causeway and new Pine Island Bridge were built. Cleveland Avenue was widened and College Parkway was built.

The opening of the Edison Mall and the relocation of the major department store from First Street were to spell a change in the character of downtown Fort Myers.

Again, construction had set new records as the 1970s opened. "Building Sets Record at $59 Million," a banner headline proclaimed. An editorial on the first day of 1970 began with a list of needs to be addressed in the coming decade: a new jail, a new city hall, a fire station on the south side, a local transit system, a new bridge from the extension of Winkler Road and a new traffic artery between and parallel to McGregor Boulevard and Cleveland Avenue.

Readers of the *News-Press* enjoyed Patrick Kelly's wry column "Only On Monday," in which he wrote in the early 1970s, "What's this spirited rivalry on West First Street? Driving east, you encounter the Ramada Inn's changeable sign: Partially Open. Welcome. Then half a block farther, you come to the Holiday Inn's changeable sign: Completely open. Welcome."

Fort Myers Mayor Oscar Corbin negotiated a contract with Fort Myers and the Lee County Nature Environmental Center to develop a nature trail and a scenic drive on the city's well field property off what was to be the Ortiz Extension.

He also worked out transactions for the sale of the land near the old train station on Peck Street to the Lee County School Board and the preservation of the rail station, which would open in the 1980s, as a historical museum.

Perhaps the most significant development of the 1970s from the standpoint of the *Fort Myers News-Press*, its readers and advertisers was its sale in October of 1971.

On Thursday morning, October 28, a front-page story revealed that "an agreement had been made for the *Fort Myers News-Press* to be acquired by the Gannett Co., the nation's largest newspaper group, with newspapers in 15 states operated under a policy of full autonomy."

The sale was in the amount of $14 million. Gannett Board Chairman Paul Miller and President Allen Neuharth flew in from corporate headquarters in Rochester, New York, to complete the deal.

These steps into the future have now become full-blown gallops. Lee County has a population of more than 253,000 and the decade of the 1980s hasn't quite reached the halfway mark.

Fort Myers remains in many ways a small town, but the future is here. Cape Coral has outpaced Fort Myers in population and Lehigh Acres is rapidly gaining. The days of street dances on First Street on Saturday nights are gone. So are the days when you could leave your car doors and front doors unlocked. Bootleg moonshine, rumrunning and cattle rustling have been supplanted by more sophisticated crimes.

And the "ears" at the top of the *News-Press* that for many years quoted Thomas A. Edison as saying, "There is only one Fort Myers and 90 million people are going to find it out" have been dropped. But its truth remains.

Originally published in the *Fort Myers News-Press* on November 21, 1984.

How Summerlin Road Got Its Name
1821

Shootouts, stampedes, town streets filled with lean, rangy cattle driven by lean, rangy cowboys…this was Fort Myers in the mid- to late 1800s. Cattle was the backbone of the area's economy and it was not uncommon for cattle to be driven down First Street through the heart of Fort Myers en route to the deep-water shipping port of Punta Rassa. The rowdy cowboys who returned from Punta Rassa to party and carouse in Fort Myers were part of the reason the little community incorporated in 1885—as proof, one of the first acts by the citizens of the newly incorporated town was to elect a town marshal to keep the high-spirited cowhands under control.

The list of men who became wealthy in the cattle business is laced with locally familiar names: Hendry, Alderman, Carlton, Lykes, Towles, Summerlin. That last name is especially well known, since chances are most motorists in Lee County will travel Summerlin Road at least once a day en route to Edison Community College, Fort Myers Beach or points south.

The man for whom the road is named is Jacob Summerlin, allegedly the first American child born near Alachua in the new territory after its formation in 1821. (Questions surround his birth; other versions report he was born February 20, 1820, in either Bartow or Lake City.) The

Jacob Summerlin. *Photo from the author's collection.*

Summerlins—who had just fought the Creek Indians in Georgia—moved from Alachua to an area called Newmansville after the Seminoles threatened to burn their homestead.

Although barely a teenager during the Seminole War, Summerlin made a name for himself as a soldier in 1835, but that was not to be his claim to historical fame. While still a young man, Summerlin inherited twenty slaves valued at $1,000 each. He bartered these for six thousand cattle and began a profitable business that would not only earn him a fortune, but a place in Florida's history books as well.

One of his earliest deals on record took place in 1854 in Orange County when Summerlin sold cattle valued at $6,500 to Robert Barnhart. Three years later, he bought 1,500 cattle for which he paid $8,150. Considering the times, these transactions were incredibly expensive.

By 1858, Summerlin was wheeling and dealing statewide. Cattleman Steve Nelson wrote of Summerlin that he had seen Jake Summerlin move 1,500 head of cattle with ten cowboys and a grub wagon all the way from St. Augustine to Tampa, Fort Myers and Punta Rassa.

Starting in north Florida, Summerlin would send a cowhand ahead to alert the ranchers that he was on the way. Those ranch owners wishing to sell their stock would start rounding them up so when Summerlin passed by, the sale could be completed quickly. Then the new acquisitions could be merged into the herd. By the time he reached Punta Rassa—which was a point of embarkation for ships headed to Cuba—his herds numbered in the thousands.

The profit was impressive. For example, a receipt dated February 4, 1854, reads "This is to show that I sold one steer for Elisabeth Whiddon for $12 and killed one as a public nisence [*sic*] as he was sick with the big head and have allowed her five dollars for him and deducted ten for…cow and a calf that I sold her that leaves a balance of seven dollars paid." Summerlin turned around and shipped the cows to Havana, Cuba. There, the cows he bought for $3 to $8 a head brought $10 to $12 in Spanish gold doublons.

When the Civil War broke out, Summerlin was already well established as a cattleman and was contracted by the Confederate government to supply beef. His contract stipulated that the Confederates would pay him eight to ten dollars per head, and he supplied approximately twenty-five thousand head between 1861 and 1863.

Under Summerlin's supervision, an estimated six hundred cattle per week were driven from the Caloosahatchee River to Baldwin, Florida, which was just south of the Georgia border. The trip was rough—it took forty days. The cowboys started off at dawn, paused during the hottest part of the day and were back on the trail by late afternoon. The average steer weighed 700 pounds at the beginning of the trip, but had dropped to 550 pounds upon arrival.

Summerlin may well have been disillusioned; as patriotic as he was at the outset of the war, he was paid in Confederate dollars that had little or no value. In 1863, he gave up his government contract and went into partnership with James McKay, a loyal Confederate from Tampa.

In December 1863, Union troops reoccupied Fort Myers, partly because acquiring beef was important to the Union army and partly to prevent the herds from reaching the Confederates. However, Summerlin and McKay had decided not to supply beef to either side.

Summerlin provided the cattle and McKay piloted his own ship, the *Scottish Chief*. They ran the Federal blockade, taking the cattle to Havana where the Spanish paid two ounces of their gold—valued at around thirty dollars—for each eight-dollar cow. On that first trip, the *Scottish Chief* carried six hundred animals.

On their return, they brought flour, sugar, salt, shoes and fabric, which they resold at phenomenal prices to the Confederates. A barrel of flour sold for $125, a sack of sugar brought $40. Because the Confederate currency was so unstable, McKay and Summerlin preferred to be paid in cattle, which the sellers drove to Boca Grande.

When the Civil War ended, Summerlin expanded his operations. Convinced that the Cuban market for range-fed cattle would last, Summerlin moved into the abandoned army barracks and began using their corrals and the wharf at Punta Rassa. Summerlin and his son, Sam, bought cattle from all over Florida, drove the herds to Punta Rassa and from there shipped them to Cuba.

At first he shipped his own cattle, but as other ranchers learned about Summerlin's port facilities, they began to bring their herds to Punta Rassa to rent the holding pens and wharf. He charged cattlemen from twenty-five to fifty cents per cow. Since the typical herd averaged two hundred head, the new sideline was quite lucrative.

By 1867, a congressional act permitted telegraph companies to take and use public lands to string lines and establish telegraph stations. The International Ocean Telegraph Co. arrived to take over the army's outpost and forced Summerlin to move. A few hundred yards upriver, he built his own wharf and a large house. He not only rented holding pens and the use of his wharf, he also rented rooms to the cowboys. For many years, Summerlin was one of the largest cattlemen in Florida. An article in the *Savannah News* in 1879 reported that Summerlin was shipping approximately ten thousand head annually.

At that point in history, banks were unstable, so many of the cattlemen kept their monies in gold, Summerlin among them. These men probably felt secure because they carried braided buckskin whips that measured twelve to eighteen feet long. The cowmen became very skilled in using the whips and some historians theorize the sound of the cracking whips led to the term "Crackers" for Southerners.

Summerlin did not make this area his permanent residence—he lived out his years in Bartow, dying there on November 4, 1893. However, as a pioneer in the cattle business, Jacob Summerlin carved a memorable place in Lee County's history.

Originally published in the July–August 1992 issue of *Lee Living*.

PUNTA RASSA
Once Capital of Cow Country, Now of Condos
1838

Chances are most people traveling to Sanibel via the causeway seldom give Punta Rassa more than a glance as they pass by or wait in line to go through the tollbooth. And yet, Punta Rassa was once far more important than Fort Myers or Sanibel.

Today Punta Rassa is the scene of rapid development, where luxurious condominiums are being constructed for wealthy retirees and vacationers. In decades past, Punta Rassa was peopled by Caloosa Indians, fishermen, soldiers and cowboys. On February 15, 1898, a telegrapher at Punta Rassa became the first person in the nation to learn that the U.S. battleship *Maine* had been sunk by the Spanish in Havana harbor, an act that would lead to the Spanish-American War. And in 1913, Punta Rassa played a role in an archaeological mystery when workmen digging shell to use in building a road uncovered the skeletons of literally dozens and dozens of Indians scattered almost at random as if they had lain where they died.

A deep-water port, Punta Rassa had been the site of Fort Dulany, established in 1838 by the U.S. Army as a supply depot during the Second Seminole War. Karl H. Grismer, writing in *The Story of Fort Myers*, described Fort Dulany as one of the best forts in south Florida. Barracks, warehouses and a hospital had been built there and Colonel

Jacob Summerlin's home at Punta Rassa, shown here in this photo taken circa 1913. By this time, Cuban demand for cattle had lessened. In 1925, the entire point, with the exception of the property where the cable station was located, had been purchased by Barron Collier, a wealthy developer. *Courtesy of the Southwest Florida Historical Museum.*

W.J. Worth, commander of federal troops in Florida, had sent many reinforcements, beefing up the manpower.

Grismer further describes the fort as "a base of operations from which troops moved into the Big Cypress and Everglades, ferreting out Indian settlements and burning them, and destroying the crops the Indians had planted."

Fort Myers was actually an afterthought and the result of a hurricane that struck on October 19, 1841, and destroyed the fort at Punta Rassa. Grismer writes that all the buildings at Fort Dulany were "demolished by the raging wind and the water which swept over the entire point, covering it many feet deep. Two soldiers were drowned. The others escaped by fleeing to higher ground before the storm reached its peak."

But Punta Rassa's claim to fame was not as the locale of an army fort. Rather, it was as a deep-water port. Joe A. Akerman Jr., in his book *Florida Cowman: A History of Florida Cattle Raising*, described Punta Rassa as "the largest cattle staging and embarkation point in the state." He explained it was ideal for picking up cattle because "vessels drawing eleven feet of water could lay within one hundred feet of the mainland."

And although there is some question as to the exact date Punta Rassa became important as a port for the shipment of cattle to Cuba, Akerman quotes from *Four Centuries of Florida Ranching* and writes that "in 1840 some 30,000 cattle were exported from Punta Rassa to Cuba."

Earlier documents pinpoint Punta Rassa as the location of a Spanish fishery. Grismer refers to a report filed in 1824 by Lieutenant Commander James M. McIntosh, captain of the U.S. schooner *Terrier*, while investigating the fishery there. "The inhabitants," McIntosh wrote, "are Spaniards and Indians. The Spaniards extensively engaged in fishing, making seines, or cultivating the soil. A considerable part…is cleared and under fine culture of corn, pumpkins and melons. There are nine neat well-thatched houses, with an extensive shed for drying fish, and a store house for their salt and provisions."

By 1858, Jake, Samuel and Clarence Summerlin (Summerlin Road was named after Jake) had arrived on the scene and were selling cattle to the Cubans.

In 1864, during the Civil War, the Union army reactivated Fort Dulany as the port from which cattle were shipped to feed the Union sailors stationed at Key West. The army constructed a barracks as well as a long wharf.

That barracks, which was later to become internationally famous as a resort for hardy sportsmen who liked to rough it, was unusual in appearance. Grismer describes it as "about a hundred feet long and fifty feet wide and gave the appearance of having been chopped in two. A row of rooms faced the water from the second floor where the other face of a roof should have been. Many years later…those rooms were jokingly dubbed 'Murderer's Row.'"

In 1866, the International Ocean and Telegraph Company moved into Punta Rassa, taking over the land and barracks under the provisions of a congressional act that permitted any telegraph company "to take and use public land necessary for the stringing of lines or the establishment of stations." Not only was there a telegraph office at Punta Rassa, it was, in fact the terminal point in the United States and the point from which 110 miles of underwater cable ran to Havana. However, International Ocean and Telegraph also controlled the port and, as Akerman writes, "controlled the shipping rights, the pens and the dock. For the use of these facilities, the company usually charged fifteen cents per cow."

C.T. Tooke, a longtime cowman and resident of Fort Myers, describes in Akerman's book the end of a typical cattle drive when the cowboys reached Punta Rassa.

> *When we got to Punta Rassa, the young fellows usually cut up a bit. They were paid off in gold and had some mighty big poker games. And they drank much more than a little Cuban rum which they got for fifty cents a gallon. It had a terrible kick and when a fellow drank a quart or so of it, he became right hilarious. Sometimes the boys got into fights, but most of them were good natured and didn't quarrel even when they were drunk.*

It was also commonly known that when the cowpokes got "liquored up," they liked to shoot and the walls and floors of the barracks were peppered with bullet holes.

George Shultz, a telegrapher from Newark, New Jersey, was in charge of the new station that was located in the old army barracks. A bright man quick to seize an opportunity, Shultz allowed cowhands to bed down in the barracks, but began serving meals for $1.50 a day.

From the standpoint of competition, Shultz had none as a hostler until 1874, when Jake Summerlin built his own hotel, the Summerlin House, a few hundred feet away.

Pioneer Captain F.A. Hendry, apparently another strong believer in private enterprise, constructed his own cow pens and a wharf at Punta Rassa and charged only ten cents a cow. These were purchased by Jake Summerlin from Hendry in 1878 for $10,000.

During the 1880s, Summerlin converted the barracks into an inn and began attracting a different following. Cows were still being shipped from Punta Rassa, but now Florida was feeling the pinch of competition from Texas and Central America. As a result, cowpunchers were being supplanted by sportsmen who came to fish the waters for kingfish, sea trout, Spanish mackerel, channel bass and tarpon.

In 1885, New York sportsman W.H. Wood—staying at the Shultzes'— landed the first tarpon ever caught with rod and reel. Prior to this, harpoon or shark hook and chain line had been used. Wood's coup made the sports pages of leading dailies around the country. So many sports fishermen came to Punta Rassa that Shultz named his inn the Tarpon House.

In 1898, when the Spanish blew up the U.S. battleship *Maine* in Havana harbor, Shultz and his assistant, W.H. McDonald, were the first people in the country to learn of the attack via the clicking telegraph keys. For the next year, the station at Punta Rassa was the most important chain in the nation's communications system. When war was declared on April 21, a home guard was organized in Fort Myers to protect the telegraph line and station from Spanish saboteurs.

By the early 1900s, Tarpon House was attracting millionaires, business magnates, political figures, titled royalty and sportsmen from around the world. The guest list was printed on the front page of the *Fort Myers Press*. Even menus were front-page news, for they detailed sumptuous feasts consisting of many courses.

As 1906 drew to a close, the Tarpon House made the front page as disaster struck. It was destroyed by a fire that left only a thirty-thousand-gallon rainwater tank standing. Western Union had acquired the ground and buildings when it absorbed International Ocean, but Shultz had made many improvements and figured his personal loss at $20,000.

Chagrined by the loss of a favorite retreat, wealthy sportsmen who had stayed at the Tarpon House helped finance Shultz so that he could rebuild. The *Fort Myers Press* reported that the new forty-room hotel that cost $40,000 to build was to open in January of 1908. The opening was a success; but alas the new hotel was also destroyed by fire in 1913 and was never rebuilt.

Years passed. Punta Rassa fell from grace as a diversion for the barons and businessmen. And then in 1927, it seemed Punta Rassa would regain its prominence, for the president of the Seaboard Air Line Railway System, S. Davies Warfield, planned to lay tracks to Punta Rassa with a view toward rebuilding Punta Rassa as a port. Warfield died before his plans could be realized and once again Punta Rassa was in limbo.

As late as 1973, *News-Press* columnist Randy White, in an article describing the village, reported a total of eleven residents. Today that is changing. The flocks of pelicans cohabit with newcomers to the area. Pleasure boats ply waters once graced by schooners. High-rises challenge the pines for air space. However, Punta Rassa's history is kept alive thanks to microfilms of old newspapers and displays such as the one at the Fort Myers Historical Museum.

Update: According to the 2000 U.S. Census, Punta Rassa had a population of 1,731 residents.

Originally published in "Only Yesterday" in the *Fort Myers News-Press* on June 24, 1984.

FORT MYERS
Lee County's Historic County Seat
1841

Fort Myers, the governmental seat of Lee County, dates its history to November 1841, when southwest Florida was embroiled in the Second Seminole War. That October, Fort Dulany, established at Punta Rassa, was destroyed by a hurricane. Captain H. McKavitt was sent upriver to find a more sheltered location. He chose the site of present-day Fort Myers, naming it Fort Harvie to honor a soldier who had died of malaria the previous September. Active for the winter, it was abandoned when hostilities with the Seminoles temporarily ceased. In 1850 a new fort was again built on the site and named Fort Myers to honor Colonel Abraham C. Myers.

Fort Myers was abandoned in 1858 following the Seminole Wars and was deserted until the Civil War, except for a brief period when it was occupied by a civil force that was studying tropical plants, wrote Captain F.A. Hendry in *A History of the Early Days in Fort Myers*. The war prompted the botanical project to be abandoned, Hendry wrote. Although Fort Myers was quite a distance from the major action of the war, the area played a prominent role as a supplier of cattle during the War Between the States.

Permanent settlers came in 1866. Soon churches, boardinghouses, saloons, livery stables and stores sprang up. The year 1884 brought a winter visitor who changed the fledgling town's future. Thomas Edison purchased a thirteen-acre tract of land and brought Mina Miller Edison,

The Fort Myers Yacht Basin. *Photo from the author's collection.*

his bride, to Fort Myers, where they honeymooned. In 1885, Fort Myers was incorporated. By 1904, Fort Myers had electric lights, a telephone system, a fire department and a railroad station. Cattle and citrus lured pioneers interested in opening a new frontier.

Working together, the citizens of Fort Myers survived the Depression, but growth was slow until World War II brought an influx of fliers. Buckingham Gunnery School trained aerial gunners and Page Field provided final training before pilots were sent overseas. Many later returned to the area to become prominent businessmen and civic leaders.

In 1947, Mrs. Edison donated the Edison Estate to the City of Fort Myers. People flocked to see the beautiful home and grounds and tourism flourished in the 1950s, along with the flower business. In the 1960s, growth escalated as more people began moving south.

In addition, the opening in 1969 of the Edison Mall lured many businesses from downtown Fort Myers south. In 1990, the Henry Ford Winter Home was opened to the public as part of the city's effort to revitalize the downtown. A quaint trolley transported visitors from the Edison and Ford Homes to the Murphy-Burroughs Home and the Fort Myers Historical Museum. Fort Myers in the 1990s was a far cry from the military outpost of 150 years earlier.

CALOOSAHATCHEE RIVER AND THE FORT MYERS YACHT BASIN

The Caloosahatchee River, named by early settlers, literally means river of the Caloosas. Emanating from the marshes near Lake Hicpochee and spanning sixty-seven miles, it reaches a depth of twenty-three feet. It was a source of food for the Caloosa Indians and, for many years before roads were built, the river was the main means of transportation. In 1850, settlers started building small shacks on the river's edge, taking fish, clams and soft-shelled turtles for food. Steamboats, carrying everything from alligator hides to tourists, made regular runs up and down the river. Lumber and prefabricated sections for Edison's home were shipped on barges to the construction site on the Caloosahatchee River. The traffic on the river, however, was not all work, as evidenced by the *Mermaid*, a floating dance hall that took revelers up and down the Caloosahatchee for an evening of music and dance.

The Fort Myers Yacht Basin was built in 1937 with $134,269 from city funds and $300,000 from the Works Progress Administration (WPA). It was enlarged in the 1970s. Today palatial yachts and sailing vessels from all over the world anchor here.

HISTORIC DOWNTOWN

Taken building by building, downtown Fort Myers's skyline is unprepossessing. However, from an architectural standpoint and when taken as a whole, the downtown is arguably the last remaining example of a 1930s Florida river town. Fort Myers is significant for still another reason. Until the Edison Mall opened in the late 1960s, Fort Myers was the social and economic center of Lee County, even though the towns and cities of Cape Coral, Lehigh Acres, Bonita Springs, Estero, Fort Myers Beach, Sanibel and Alva also existed. Everyone living in Lee County traveled to Fort Myers to shop and do business. As a result, the majority of Lee County's early history took place in Fort Myers. That's why the businesses and buildings that remain are important.

First Street is appropriately named, since it is the city's oldest street. Cattlemen on horseback drove their herds down the street, kicking up dust en route to Punta Rassa, a deep-water port where the cattle were shipped to Cuba. By 1910, First Street was lined with a ladies' trading place, a hotel, dry goods stores and a book and music store. Cornmeal spread on the hard shell road made a fine dance floor on Saturday nights for those who came

The Morgan Hotel, now known as the Dean Hotel. *Courtesy of the Southwest Florida Historical Museum.*

to town. Parades have always been a favorite pastime and First Street has had them all. Today First Street is still the main parade route for the annual festivities honoring Thomas Edison, including the Grand Parade.

Shopping malls have taken their toll on the retail stores on First Street, but office buildings, along with historic preservation and renovation, are revitalizing the area. Live theater in the Arcade, block parties, trolley rides, craft shows and nightclubs are bringing new life to the area.

Bay Street, one block north of First Street, is first seen on the city plats of 1914 when it was one block long running between Hendry and Jackson Streets along what was then the riverbank. By 1926, it spanned four blocks from Riverview (now Citrus) to Lee Street, giving access to the docks that extended out into the Caloosahatchee River. Gulf Refining Company, Raymond & Company and Lee County Packing Company used the docks. The railroad cut across the end of Bay Street out onto the Lee County Packinghouse dock to expedite their shipments of produce. Bay Street now runs from Centennial Park, merging into First Street, for a distance of about a half-mile.

Once part of a large city recreation complex, the **Hall of Fifty States** on the southeast corner of Hendry Street was completed in 1927 at a cost of almost $48,000 and served as the focal point of the Moorish-style Pleasure Pier that jutted over the Caloosahatchee River where the bridge is now. For nearly two decades, it was the place to take your girl dancing, to hear concerts, talent shows or political speeches. The pier was torn down in 1943, but the auditorium was hoisted to its present location, where it became a social center (USO) for servicemen training here during the Second World War. Today, as the Hall of Fifty States, it is part of the city-owned Tourist Center.

The **Morgan Hotel** was opened in 1924 with its main entrance and brass-railed front porch fronting on First Street. Built by Rhode Island developer John Morgan Dean, it advertised sixty-two rooms with sixty-two baths, telephone booths in the lobby and a dining room with a solarium on the roof. Before Dean transformed the wooden Sanchez boardinghouse into his namesake hotel, he got the city's approval to open Dean Street. The name of the hotel was changed to Hotel Dean in the 1970s when the building was purchased by Sam Johnston Sr.

The **Franklin Arms**, located at the southwest corner of First and Lee Streets, was hailed as the first skyscraper on Florida's west coast south of Tampa when built in 1913. The hotel was built by W.P. Franklin and boasted 102 steam-heated rooms, a roof garden with a pergola and a rooftop restaurant after an eight-story addition was completed in 1924 at a cost of $120,000. During the real estate boom in the 1920s, a "human fly" hustled up the tall hotel, stopping at each floor to tell the gaping spectators below to hurry up and buy a piece of a new subdivision called Palmlee Park. The landmark was acquired by Gilmer Heitman in 1935. About 1975, it was given a facelift and a new name: the Edison Regency Hotel.

Built by Harvie B. Heitman, the **Bradford Hotel** on First Street was financed by Fort Myers benefactor Tootie McGregor Terry and named in honor of her only son, Bradford, who died at a very young age. The brick hotel opened November 12, 1905, boasting forty-one rooms and a large dining room on the second floor. The Bradford catered to visiting sportsmen, which meant guests had to be careful walking down the halls at night because hunters often tied their hunting dogs to the doorknobs. By the 1940s, the Bradford had expanded to one hundred rooms and had a dining room on the first floor facing First Street. In the late 1930s, Heitman sold the hotel to former Fort Myers Mayor David G. Shapard, who operated it until the 1970s. Local appliance dealer Bill Smith bought the venerable building in 1979. Today it houses a law firm on the first floor and rental apartments on the second and third.

Down the street from the Bradford is the **Arcade Theater**, where Thomas Edison is said to have enjoyed silent movies. (Being deaf he had an advantage in being able to read the actors' lips. He was never as fond of "talkies.") Built by the Heitman brothers, Gilmer and Harvie, around 1915, the brick theater was part of the Arcade development and looked much as it does today, although it was narrower. Local residents remember it used to flood during hurricanes. It was widened and remodeled in the 1920s. However, the theater has always been where it is and many businesses through the years have occupied the stores that span the Arcade walkthrough. The theater was the scene of early stage shows featuring vaudeville, magic acts and local talent nights, which is why the stage is wider and deeper than most movie houses. In the 1970s, it was closed to movies and used by area amateur theater groups. Its stage is now used by the Department of Cultural Affairs for children's enrichment programs and live theatrical productions.

The **Edison Theater** at the northeast corner of Main and Hendry Streets was built in 1940–41 when its modified Art Deco style of architecture was much in vogue. The lobby and the restrooms were ornate and the stadium entrance inside gave the feeling of a balcony. Popular with servicemen stationed here during World War II, it boasted live entertainment on its stage.

Today known as the **Marketplace**, originally the building on First Street near the southwest corner of Jackson Street was known as the Langford Building/Bank of Fort Myers. During 1911, Taff O. Langford built this two-story brick structure sandwiched between the new Bank of Fort Myers on the east and a livery stable on the west. Two years later, John T. Hendry established the first public picture show in town here. Called the Grand Theater, it featured pictures approved by the Board of Censors as morally clean. In 1915, volunteer firemen, aided by townspeople, saved the building from a fire that threatened the entire block. J.C. Penney and Diana Shops were both located in the building at one time. During World War II, the Rendezvous was located right on the corner and was a favorite hot spot for servicemen. After Bill Smith purchased the brick building, he renovated and transformed it into the mini-mall Marketplace, which includes the French Connection Restaurant.

Diagonally across from the French Connection is what is known at this writing as the **George W. Whitehurst Federal Building**, situated on First Street between Jackson and Lee Streets. Until 1965, you could stop by this block-wide post office and pick up your mail from the open-air lockboxes any time of day or night. When completed in 1933, the $200,000 structure was acclaimed as the most attractive post office in any city of this size in America. The beauty came not only from the classic design but also from the building material, for it was constructed of coral formations, seashells and limestone quarried in the Florida Keys. The post office, a WPA project,

45

The U.S. Post Office under construction in 1933. The photo was taken in July, before the post office opened. Across the street (far right) was the Franklin Arms Hotel. *Courtesy of the Southwest Florida Historical Society.*

was constructed within the site of the original fort built during the Seminole Wars—unquestionably the most historic spot in Lee County. In 1982, the building was remodeled for use as a federal courthouse and named to honor Judge Whitehurst, the man credited as being responsible for the creation of the Middle District of the U.S. Court.

In 1934, Fort Myers's only granite "edifice" was erected as the new home of the **First National Bank**, diagonally across the street from the Bradford Hotel. The community center known as Phoenix Hall sat on this corner before the bank was built. The building has floors of Italian marble and cost $50,000 to construct. The façade and the interior are staid and ornate, but the business deals transacted inside its walls were often simple, straightforward and sealed not with a notary's stamp, but a handshake. Today the restored building contains the offices of the law firm of Bigelow and Winesett.

A block south of the First National Bank is the **Lee County Bank** at the northwest corner of Main and Hendry Streets. Built in 1911 by James A. "Pineapple Jim" Hendry as a general store, this two-story building was constructed of heart pine and housed the Fort Myers Post Office for years. Once, when the Caloosahatchee River overflowed during a tropical storm, patrons rowed to their boxes to pick up their mail. The red brick exterior was stuccoed in 1927 when it became the home of the Lee County Bank. The bank remodeled the structure again in 1951 and a large mosaic of General Robert E. Lee astride his horse Traveler was reproduced in colorful tile on the recessed wall facing Hendry Street.

Catty-cornered from the former First National Bank at the northwest corner of First and Hendry Streets is **Heritage Square**. Formerly known as the Heitman-Evans Building, the original building was built as a general store by Jehu Blount around 1874. As the town's first unofficial postmaster (he received no pay), Blount carved a slot for mail in the side of his general store during the pioneer times. Then, in 1914, Harvie Heitman tore down the forty-year-old dilapidated building and constructed a modern store. For years a hardware and farm implement store occupied this corner building and, later, Belk Lindsey Department Store. In 1975, Bruce J. Scott bought the time-honored building with its twelve-inch-thick walls and high, stamped-metal ceilings and transformed it into a quaint mall. To preserve a bit of the history of old Fort Myers, Scott used tough heart pine timbers, antique bricks and big windowpanes from the demolished Crescent Building on Second Street, once the Fort Myers Junior High School.

Two of the oldest homes in Fort Myers have been transformed into what is arguably Fort Myers's finest restaurant—**The Veranda**. Located at the corner of Second and Broadway, the front of the restaurant is actually the kitchen of the former Gonzalez house, built in 1912 by Manuel Gonzalez. Manuel was the son of Nanny Gonzalez, who came to Fort Myers in 1866 and was one the first settlers. In 1973, Peter Pulitzer (grandson of the newspaper mogul) purchased the house, which then faced Broadway. The house was turned so the porch led into the courtyard and was connected to the adjacent J. Franklin Garner house. The Garner house, fronting on Second Street at the Broadway intersection, still stands where it was built about 1902.

As the county seat, it is only fitting that homage should be paid in Fort Myers to **General Robert E. Lee**, the man for whom Lee County is named, and this has been done in the form of a bronze bust. The bust of Lee was placed on Monroe Street and is a monument to persistence as well. The United Daughters of the Confederacy (UDC) decided to take as their first fundraising project a statue to honor the soldier and statesman for whom Lee County was named. Unfortunately, the funds raised had to be diverted for more immediate needs, including Lee Memorial Hospital, which opened in 1916. The bust was finally erected in 1966 as the culmination of a project begun in 1913 by the Letitia Chapter of the UDC. The completed artwork has a granite base, is one and a half times life size, measures ten and a half feet tall and cost $6,000.

Twenty-two years later in October 1988, at the Florida Panther Jamboree, a bronze sculpture by Don Wilkins was unveiled in front of the U.S. Post Office. The life-size panther family, a cub with his parents, lolls in a sixty-nine-foot-long flowerbed and is a "hands on" sculpture that both children and adults love to touch. Across Edwards Drive in Centennial Park is another Wilkins sculpture titled *Uncommon Friends*. Completed in February 1990, it depicts Henry Ford, Thomas Edison and Harvey Firestone relaxing around a campfire in the Florida wilderness.

Originally published by Prudy's Press in 1990.

THE SANIBEL LIGHT
A Beacon for Mariners
1884

For more than a century, the rays of the Sanibel Light, like the fingers of a helping hand, have stretched across the waters of the Gulf of Mexico to guide thousands of ships and seamen to safety and civilization. Since 1884, the light has functioned as a beacon. Today sunbathers, artists and amateur photographers far outnumber the ships and appreciate the light not for its usefulness, but for its picturesque charm.

However, the light is more than a subject for artists, more than a navigational aid for boaters. It is a relic of Sanibel's colorful history and beyond that can be regarded as a symbol of man's determination—it took persistence to get the light built and, in recent years, persistence to keep it.

Settlers on Sanibel first petitioned the U.S. government for a light in December of 1833 because ship traffic in the Gulf was steadily increasing. However, the petition was unsuccessful, perhaps in part because Sanibel was to be deserted within a few years and no one remained to follow through.

BUREAUCRATIC SHUFFLES

The next appeal was filed December 10, 1856, by the US. Light House Board, a relatively new federal agency responsible for the establishment and operation of lighthouses. (The board, which replaced the U.S. Lighthouse Establishment created in 1789, had been formed in 1851 during the administration of President Millard Fillmore.) This petition called for reserving the entire island for lighthouse purposes, but was apparently lost in a bureaucratic shuffle, for there is no record that any action was taken.

Then, according to local historian Florence Fritz, a district engineer employed by the Light House Board petitioned Secretary of the Treasury John Sherman to obtain the title to "Land Requested in 1856."

Sanibel resident and historian Elinor Dormer writes in *The Seashell Islands* that the General Land Office acted within nine days and on January 9, 1878, Sanibel was closed to private ownership.

NEED GROWS CRITICAL

By this time, the need for a light had grown critical. A lighthouse had been built at Egmont Key near Tampa in 1848, but there was no light between Key West and Tampa. In the intervening years, Punta Rassa, then a deep-water port, had become the point from which cattle were being shipped to both Cuba and Spain. As a result, it bustled with activity. Then, too, general shipping traffic between Key West and other ports along the Gulf Coast had been growing.

In her book *The Unknown Story of World Famous Sanibel and Captiva*, Fritz points to the danger to ships that existed when she writes, "Point Ybel could not be seen in the dark so ships had to be piloted by instinct and long experience to anchor in Carlos Bay."

The Light House Board recommended $40,000 be set aside for construction of the Sanibel Light and in 1881, Congress passed an act authorizing its erection. However, even at this point, the light's construction was by no means assured. In 1882 a memo was discovered that indicated islands set aside for lighthouses had been "withdrawn by letter from the General Land Office."

This was remedied and in April of 1883, the Light House Board engineer surveyed Sanibel and forty-two acres composing the east end of the island were reserved. Later, the entire island was reserved to guard against future erosion. Congress approved the plan and $50,000 was set aside.

Still another bureaucratic problem surfaced: it was now determined that the land did not belong to the federal government, but rather to the State of Florida by virtue of the Swamp Lands Act of 1850. A representative of the Department of the Interior wrote Governor W.D. Bloxham requesting that Florida relinquish title to the proposed site, which the governor did in August of 1883.

CONSTRUCTION BEGINS

On August 29, 1883, a contract with the Phoenix Iron Company was signed in which Phoenix was to furnish the metal work for the lighthouse, and construction commenced in February 1884. The first stage of its construction was a wharf, 162 feet long, with a T-head 30 by 60 feet, built on creosoted pilings.

Still another delay arose. The ship bearing the metal works for the lighthouse wrecked and sank only miles from Point Ybel. According to the report of the Light House Board, "The L.H. Engineer with the crews and working party from the tenders 'Arbutus' and 'Mignonette' and a diver, afterwards fished up all of the wrecked iron and landed it on the wharf at Sanibel Island, with the exception of two small gallery brackets, duplicates of which were afterwards made in New Orleans. Owing to this delay the station, will not be completed until some time in August."

The lighthouse was finally completed and activated August 20, 1884. Also built at that time were the two detached frame houses positioned on iron columns.

When completed, the light looked almost exactly as it does today with the exception that the light source changed. The light was 98 feet above sea level, the tower 104 feet. It was a skeleton iron structure in the shape of a frustum or base of a four-sided pyramid. The ironwork surrounded a circular cylinder 20 feet off the ground, which contained a spiral stairway made up of 127 steps enabling the keepers to reach the light. At the top was the iron watch room and, above that, the lantern. Each had a separate railing.

The huge lens was known as a Fresnel, named after Augustin J. Fresnel, the French physicist and engineer who designed this type of lens specifically for lighthouses. It was described as an echelon lens, a compound lens consisting of annular or ring-shaped lenses arranged about a central lens so that all have a common focus, which increases both the intensity and the range of the light produced.

When first built and fueled by coal oil, the lens had a range of $15^{3}/_{4}$ nautical miles and was a white light varied by a white flash every two minutes.

According to the U.S. Coast Guard light list, the Sanibel Light's normal range was thirteen miles and it was a group flashing light, which means it flashed off .05 seconds, on 1.5 seconds, off .05 seconds and on 7.5 seconds in ten-second sequences.

FIRST TENDER ARRIVES

Dudley Richardson, the first lighthouse keeper, came from Key West with his assistant, John Johnson. Richardson was officially appointed on November 24, 1884, and Johnson served until 1890, when he was replaced by Henry Shanahan, who had arrived on Sanibel in 1888, sailing from Key West in a sailboat with his wife and two sons. Shanahan became keeper in 1892 when Richardson resigned.

Shanahan's salary was $740 annually, an impressive amount for the times. His son, Eugene, was appointed his assistant and received $600. They earned their pay.

Taking care of the light was never easy. The original light had a large wick that had to be continually trimmed and watched. According to Clarence Rutland in a 1970 interview, the light was changed in 1912 to oil vapor, but even that required constant tending.

Rutland, who died in 1982 at ninety-one, was an excellent source of information concerning the light. Not only was he Henry Shanahan's stepson, he was also employed as assistant light keeper from 1918 through 1926 and again from 1936 through 1941.

MOSQUITOES MEASURED IN GALLONS

Residents and visitors to Sanibel will appreciate the comfort of the island life today when they compare it to conditions Rutland described when he said,

> *Back in those days you could take a quart can and catch a gallon of mosquitoes.*
>
> *There were two men there at the time* [referring to his first term as assistant lighthouse keeper]. *We changed watch each night at 12. It was an oil light then and we'd take a five-gallon can up full in the afternoon and pump the light and bring the can down empty in the morning.*
>
> *The light had clockworks with weights on it and you had to keep that flashing to the second. Somebody had to be with it almost every minute. During the day, we had curtains we hung around every one of those prisms.*

MANY NEEDS SERVED

For years as Sanibel Island dozed in the sun, accessible to visitors only by ferry, the lighthouse and its keepers maintained the vigil. Not only did the two frame houses next to the tower serve as shelter to the lighthouse keepers and their families, but during hurricanes they were a sanctuary for islanders who sought refuge as well. During Prohibition the nearby inlets and mangrove-lined bays served as escape routes for local moonshiners and rumrunners fleeing federal revenue agents. In 1952, a TV antenna was attached to the lighthouse, providing the first television reception for the locals.

The light and its operation remained basically unchanged until 1939, when President Franklin D. Roosevelt placed the operation and the maintenance of all lighthouses under the protective wing of the U.S. Coast Guard, where they remain at this writing. This did not immediately affect the Sanibel Light, which had been placed under the coast guard's jurisdiction by an executive order in 1883. However, the threat of war did mean that while civilian lighthouse keepers remained on duty, coast guard personnel were transferred in and stationed at the lighthouse as well.

Modern Improvements

Bowing to advances in technology, the Sanibel Light was again converted in the early 1940s—this time using acetylene gas as a fuel. Furthermore, the light was turned on and off by a sun valve triggered by a photoelectric cell reacting to the absence of light.

W.R. England Jr. was the light keeper from 1946 through 1949. He was one of the servicemen transferred to Sanibel and was chief bosun's mate. Interviewed by this author in March 1970, he remembered the acetylene light well.

"Every morning," he said, "we would go up, put the curtains up and clean the lens and the big light. In the evenings, we would take the curtains down. We used to have to change the tanks. There were six tanks of acetylene hooked up together and I know those tanks weighed 225 pounds each."

England and his wife closed the light as an attended station in April of 1949, but the buildings were not idle. In 1950 they functioned as headquarters for the J.N. Ding Darling National Wildlife Refuge until March of 1982 when the refuge built its own building on refuge grounds.

Acceding again to technology, the light was converted to electricity in 1962, using a 250-watt bulb and commercial power. Then, for the first time in its history, the Sanibel Light was dark because of the failure of a mercury switch. After a number of outages, one lasting a week, the light was finally repaired and once again brightened Sanibel waters.

Ten years later, however, in October of 1972, the coast guard announced the light would be shut down unless its usefulness could be justified. In a front-page story in the October 20, 1972 issue of the *Fort Myers News-Press*, reporter Lee Melsek quoted the captain of the coast guard as saying cost of operation wasn't a concern. "It costs only a few dollars a month to keep the light on and about $2,500 or $3,500 to sandblast and paint the structure every 10 years."

SAFE AT LAST

At the public hearing, citizens, boaters and fishermen convinced the coast guard the light was still useful and it was granted a "stay of execution." Far-sighted people, however, saw to it that the Sanibel Light and keepers' quarters were listed on the National Register of Historic Places the following November. Historically the buildings are significant because they are the oldest on Sanibel Island.

As southwest Florida continues to experience the incredible growth that has had so tremendous an impact, it is reassuring that such an important part of Sanibel's past has been preserved and remains to inspire artists and to guide both sunbathers and mariners.

Originally published in 1990 by Prudy's Press.

St. James City and a Once Grand Hotel
1885

S t. James-on-the-Gulf...a name that once quickened the pulses and
purses of four developers from Maine. The financial foursome included
E.C. Nichols, Charles A. Boardman, James Kreamer and E. Whiteside. On
May 16, 1885, they affixed their signatures to the Articles of Incorporation
that created the St. James Company.

The company's "object and business," according to these articles, was
"the acquirement...of lands in the State of Florida, the development of
Pine Island in Monroe County, Florida, the building of a large city on said
Pine Island, building wharves, chartering and running vessels in the interest
of commerce." The new firm was capitalized in the amount of $75,000.

The "large city" was what is known today as St. James City, which is
located at the southernmost tip of Pine Island. Pine Island had been surveyed
for homesteading in 1879, a scant six years prior to the incorporation of St.
James. Actually, St. James is three months older than the city of Fort Myers,
which was incorporated August 12, 1885.

According to the book *The Unknown Story of World Famous Sanibel and
Captiva* by Florence Fritz, the promoters began setting out thousands of
coconut palms, orange trees and banana plants at once. They also launched
an advertising campaign and constructed a dock on high pilings along with
a store and post office. Their most noteworthy project was the building of

the three-story, frame San Carlos Hotel that became the social center of the islands during those early years. It was constructed with fifty rooms and a dining room that could seat one hundred diners.

In another book that is invaluable to any aficionado of southwest Florida's history, a party is described that was held in the winter of 1896–97 at the San Carlos Hotel. In that book, *Florida's Vanishing Era* by Eleanor H.D. Pearse, the author tells of the three black musicians who provided the music. One played the harmonica, one kept rhythm by pounding on the floor with two sticks and the third blew into an empty bottle. What the party lacked in polish, however, was compensated for by the enthusiasm of the guests. The party, according to Pearse, didn't get started until after midnight and didn't end until after 4:00 a.m.

Why, you might ask, did the party get such a late start? According to Pearse, the only mode of transportation between the islands was a sailboat. The wind died down around sunset and they had to wait until it freshened to travel.

Pearse's father, Charles A. Dean, had first visited Pine Island and the San Carlos Hotel during the winter of 1887–88. He was so intrigued by the tropical foliage that he sent his daughter a box containing prickly pears, air plants and later oleander. At the time of his visit, the hotel was run by a Mr. Bemis. You could only reach Pine Island by boat and, once at the dock, you were taken to the hotel by a horse-drawn wagonette or "herdic" over a long, winding road of white seashells. To reach Pine Island, Dean had traveled from Jacksonville on a small steamer that Charles Boardman, one of the incorporators, had hired for his family.

Dean mentions the nightlife as being virtually nonexistent. Except for special occasions, everyone was in bed by nine o'clock. Typically, the summer population of Pine Island numbered about 50, but that winter, the population had swelled to 125, counting hotel staff and visitors.

In its heyday, St. James and the San Carlos Hotel were host to some of the country's leading citizens. Thomas Alva Edison, who had bought his Fort Myers home in March of 1885, visited. So did Henry Ford, Harvie Firestone and President Theodore Roosevelt. Roosevelt had been drawn to the area because of its excellent tarpon fishing.

The St. James-on-the-Gulf Company managed to keep going until the early 1900s, when it finally went under. In 1905, a group from the Koreshan Unity colony at Estero purchased the San Carlos Hotel. According to Allen H. Andrews, a member of the group, they also bought the hotel annex and the big wooden dock. It had been closed for several seasons and repairs were necessary.

Andrews recounts what happened next in his book *A Yank Pioneer in Florida*. It seems that a crew of workmen had been brought from Estero to prepare

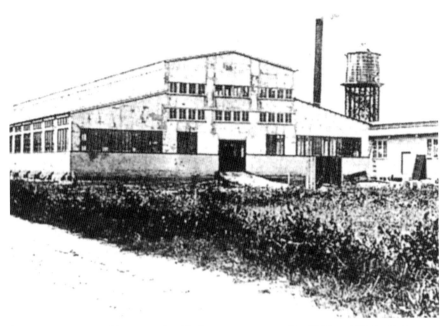

Hemp was processed into rope in this factory constructed in 1912 or 1913 in St. James City on the southernmost tip of Pine Island. In addition to building the factory, Sisal Hemp & Development Co. built a new hotel, an ice plant and a power plant in St. James City. *Courtesy of the Southwest Florida Historical Museum.*

the hotel for reopening. At quitting time on the night of July 27, 1905, a careless workman left a lighted smudge pot inside the hotel. (The smudge pots were being used to repel mosquitoes.) The hotel was set on fire and burned to the ground in a spectacular blaze. The Koreshan Unity later sold both the annex and the dock.

After being virtually deserted for six years, in 1911 St. James became the scene of new activity. The Sisal Hemp & Development Company from the Bahama Islands bought the property and planted acres of *sansieveria*, a species of hemp. The *sansieveria* was to be used to make rope.

In conjunction with this new venture, the company built a new San Carlos Hotel, an ice plant and a power plant. Storage rooms were built on the dock to hold the hemp prior to shipping. Alas, financial success was just not in the cards for the hemp business. Before long the hemp entrepreneurs learned that hemp could be grown much cheaper in Yucatan where wages were much, much lower. By 1915, this latest scheme had become only a memory.

During the intervening years, time and weather took their merciless toll on the hotel. The original store and dock were destroyed in a hurricane and a second store was built. Today, all that remains is a series of concrete pilings that straggle out from the land. The store building still stands, but has been covered over with shingles and is being used for storage. The grounds where the once grand San Carlos Hotel stood are today the site of the Shangri-La Mobilehome Park.

Update: According to the U.S. Census of 2000, 4,105 people called St. James City home.

Originally published in the February 1979 issue of *Lee Living*.

THE DEVASTATING FIRE THAT FORMED LEE COUNTY
1886

Fire! This force of nature that evokes panic and a sense of desperation in people around the world was the harbinger—in a backhanded sense—of good for early Lee Countians. To be more precise, it is because of the schoolhouse fire on May 12, 1886, that Lee County was formed.

At this point in our history, Fort Myers was in Monroe County and Key West was the county seat. When the Fort Myers Academy burned, a delegation from Fort Myers traveled by boat to Key West to appear before the Monroe County commissioners. The commissioners' attitude was that Fort Myers should have taken better care of its school. The bottom line was that there was no tax money for construction of a new academy. Enflamed, the local folks returned angry and determined to form a new county that would be more responsive to the needs of its citizens. Lee County was formed the following year.

While civic leaders might have appreciated the importance of a school facility and the necessity of creating Lee County, perhaps the most significant object lesson to be derived from the fire escaped them. That was, of course, the importance of providing fire protection.

To be fair, the area was sparsely populated; in 1900, the census recorded 943 residents of Fort Myers and 3,071 in Lee County. And fires weren't that common. But when a major blaze erupted, the populace was helpless.

And that's just what happened on May 2, 1901. The last fire of any magnitude had occurred twelve years earlier so no one was really prepared when fire broke out in the kitchen of a home in downtown Fort Myers owned by Mrs. Carrie Bass. Living there was Dr. W.B. Winkler, who was also operating a steam laundry on the premises.

According to newspaper reports and research done by Fort Myers's Assistant Fire Chief Don Stonestreet, Miss Annie Hill was visiting Mrs. Winkler when the fire was discovered. The ladies heard a crackling noise in the kitchen and when they investigated discovered the stovepipe had caught fire.

Weather conditions, fortunately, were not a contributing factor. The wind was not strong and was from the wrong direction. The fire developed slowly and, at first, it looked as though the home might be saved. The neighbors labored diligently, carrying out the furniture from the first floor and even the laundry equipment. Alas, the supply of water was inadequate to quell the flames. Within half an hour, the fire was out of control.

While flames consumed the Bass house, concern veered to the neighboring homes. Frantic citizens repositioned the bucket brigade to douse the houses so the fire wouldn't spread. When the peril had passed, it was obvious the damage was devastating. The loss to Mrs. Bass—she was not insured—of the house and citrus trees was estimated to be $2,000, a fortune in those days. The Winklers lost their bedroom furniture, their clothing and nearly all of Mrs. Winkler's jewelry. Their loss amounted to $500, another healthy sum.

That fire pointed to still another irony. The water for the bucket brigades had to be pumped from wells, for Fort Myers had no water system. Barely two weeks earlier, the council had voted down a $10,000 bond issue that designated $3,000 for street improvements and $7,000 for a water system.

The following day, May 3, 1901, a truly disastrous fire nearly decimated the city of Jacksonville. The story of the Jacksonville fire was reported in the same issue of the newspaper as the Bass fire. The blaze broke out in the Cleveland Fibre Factory and by the time it was under control, 135 blocks had burned, 10,000 people were homeless and the losses totaled between $10 and $15 million.

The news of Jacksonville's misfortune sent shock waves shivering through our small community, which rallied at once by launching a drive to raise money to send to the needy in Jacksonville.

But Fort Myers also got the clear message: they desperately, urgently needed fire protection. Immediate steps were taken to form Fort Myers's first fire department. Thirty men met Monday, May 6, 1901, at Travers Hall downtown. A committee was appointed to draft bylaws for the Fort Myers Volunteer Fire Department and C.F. Roberts was elected chief.

The firefighters met again May 13, 1901, and elected permanent officers. More than that, they voted to purchase a hand-operated fire engine and a committee was appointed to raise the money to pay for it. The community responded quickly. More than $500 was raised the first day. Winter residents helped as well. From his New Jersey home, Thomas Edison pledged $50.

Alas, before they even had a chance to get organized, fire struck again. The very next day, May 14, Captain and Mrs. Robert Lilly's home was destroyed by a fire that broke out about 5:30 that afternoon. Captain Lilly had been walking home when he saw flames and smoke gushing out of the second-floor windows of his home. He ran to the Baptist church and rang the bell.

According to the newspaper reporter's account, "Almost at first tap, it seemed that every one in town started for the fire, for although it is a common thing to hear the church bell ring, all seemed to feel that this meant fire. In less time than it takes to describe it, men had gathered at the scene of the fire from all parts of town."

The fire burned too rapidly to save the house, especially when what was needed was a strong stream of water as opposed to hand-conveyed buckets. The men focused their efforts on saving the Lillys' furniture. They were partially successful. The fire was too fierce for them to salvage the furnishings on the second floor. And still another unfortunate note, the Lillys' insurance had lapsed the previous month so they, too, were uninsured.

In the meantime, the hard-pressed firefighters had turned their attention to the Eli Pool cottage, which was adjacent to the Lilly property. By keeping the house soaked with water, they prevented the flames from spreading. However, while they were occupied with the Pool home, the Baptist church across the street began to smoke and catch fire.

The firefighters, joined now by women and children, labored fiercely and when the danger had passed, the church was safe and there were no reported injuries, except for many aching backs and shoulders.

After not suffering any serious fires in twelve years, Fort Myers had suffered two in as many weeks. As a result, the summer of 1901 was not only long and hot, but tense as well. The entire town was relieved on August 12 when the secondhand fire engine ordered from the Bainbridge, Georgia Fire Department arrived onboard the USS *Caloosa*.

According to *The History of the Fort Myers Fire Department* compiled by Don Stonestreet, the "button hand pumper had been used very little and was found to be in first class condition. The engine was connected to the Roberts well and with only eight men pumping, a good stream of water was thrown to the top of C.F. Cates' Wagon Shop, a height of 30 feet. The engine came equipped with 250 feet of hose, 15 feet of suction hose and nozzles."

Meanwhile, Cates, who was also a member of the newly formed volunteer fire department, had been making a hook and ladder truck and it was finished about the time the fire engine arrived. Although the new fire equipment would not be called into service until December of 1902, Fort Myers residents felt secure and the town itself had taken one giant step into the twentieth century.

Originally published in the May–June 1992 issue of *Lee Living*.

AND THERE WAS LIGHT
IN LEE COUNTY
1887

The year was 1887, the month March. Within days, Lee County would be created by an act of the state legislature, carved from Monroe County. The about-to-be-born county had a population of 1,414, according to the census, and this included today's Hendry and Collier Counties.

Thomas Edison had arrived for the season and the *Fort Myers Press*, reprinting a news story from another paper, informed its readers that "Mr. Edison...was playing havoc with the fish. It is said that he runs a wire out on the bottom of the gulf or river and electrifies all the fish that come near and they rise to the surface dead." And the *Press* shared news of a scientific discovery when it reported, "Fish thus electrified keep indefinitely without ice."

Electricity was very much on everyone's mind and in the Thursday, March 26 edition of the *Press*, an article was reprinted from the *American Agriculturist* that described the area. "In spite of its prominence," the reporter wrote, "it is a very small town, having less than 300 [and here the *Press* editor inserted "over 500"] inhabitants and no railroad within many miles...so far in advance of civilization over anything in the way of a frontier town as to cause comment...The people are all intelligent, educated and moral. There are no saloons and they have crushed out every bad element."

In this innocent paradise, the article continued, "Edison...pursues his experiments in electricity. His villa and grounds are lighted with electric light. Recently he offered to light the town…if the citizens would contribute the funds to put up the poles and wire, which they did, and now the road leading to his house, as well as the little village, is nightly illuminated as brightly as any place in New York."

These details were imparted by Major B.S. Henning, an orange grove owner from New York, and they were a tad premature. It wasn't until three days later, on March 27, that the lights were turned on for the first time at Seminole Lodge, Edison's home.

It was a Saturday and the residents were impressed. Nearly everyone in town managed to find their way to Edison's home that evening to observe the spectacle. In part, the excitement was increased because Edison had promised the previous March that he would provide streetlights for the entire town.

In fact, the April 21 edition of the *Press* reported that "the dynamo to be used in lighting the town of Fort Myers by electricity arrived one day last week."

The *Press* continued, "As Mr. Edison is very busy and his stay short, we have our doubts as to whether he will light Fort Myers by electricity this year or not…However, the plant will be put in good season next winter and we'll all rejoice."

It was not to be. When Edison left that May, he would not return to Fort Myers until 1901 and it was not until 1898 that Fort Myers would have electricity. And then it was not through Edison's efforts, but those of a local businessman, A.A. Gardner.

As Karl H. Grismer wrote in *The Story of Fort Myers*, Gardner had long been interested in setting up an electric plant to operate in conjunction with his canning firm, Seminole Canning. Gardner had approached local citizens and merchants in 1892 and they had indicated their support, but the country's economic problems the following year put the project on the back burner.

Then, late in the summer of 1897, Hugh O'Neill entered the local business scene. Described by Grismer as "one of the leading merchant princes of the nation, being the owner of H. O'Neill & Co., a New York department store which occupied an entire block on Sixth Avenue and employed 1,800 persons," O'Neill wintered at the Tarpon House at Punta Rassa for four years. Now he decided he would build a resort hotel.

O'Neill had intended to build his own generator, but Gardner approached him and he agreed to become Gardner's first customer. The *Fort Myers Press* was filled in the months that followed with stories about the new tourist hotel, but little was written about the forthcoming power plant. However, Gardner applied to the Fort Myers City Council for a franchise, which he received October 9, 1897. The franchise was for a term of five years and the City was to pay Gardner $300 a year for ten thirty-two-candlepower incandescent streetlights.

As for the hotel, it was to be constructed at the foot of Royal Palm Avenue on the site of the former Hendry House, a twelve-room hotel. The *Fort Myers Press* describes the lighting of the proposed hotel in its September 16 edition:

> *The house and verandas are to be lighted with electric lights throughout of the best make. The large rooms will have center lights from the ceiling, which will be turned on by a patent switchboard at the doors. The small rooms will have lights on the side of the wall to be turned on by hand. The lights in the halls and verandas will be turned on by a switchboard in the office. Altogether there will be 212 electric lights.*

In the December 30, 1897 edition of the *Press*, it was reported that the town would have lights as of that Saturday, "and if everything works satisfactory [*sic*] the electric lights will be used regularly commencing next Monday night. The dynamo is registered as a 480-revolution machine, 75 amperes, and 250 volts generating electricity for about 400 watts of 16 candle power."

An indication that Fort Myers was only a doorstep away from the wilderness is revealed by a tongue-in-cheek news item in that same edition. It seems a local man, Mr. R. Ingram O. Travers, had been advertising in the *Press* for a seven-foot alligator and had withdrawn the ad.

> *One big saurian was brought to his house on Tuesday night and several other parties have notified him that they had seven-foot pets ready to deliver to him. He is not opening a menagerie, but wanted one 'gator to keep the dogs and coons out of his grounds. He says he fears that if the knowledge that $10 may be gotten for a seven-foot gator in Myers [sic] is spread he may awake some morning to find the whole Seminole tribe standing at his gate with a "bunch" of gators large enough to knock out his bank account in the first round.*

But civilization was definitely making inroads. In the next edition of the paper, sharing headlines with a hunting party that claimed to have spotted 109 deer in only a few days and a poem by a local anonymous poet entitled "Fort Myers After the Last Frost" was the story headlined "Fort Myers Has Electric Lights."

The brief story recounted the events of the previous Saturday when at dusk

> *a bright, soft light suddenly appeared in all the stores and houses connected with the electric light plant, and for the first time electricity was used as a lighting power in Lee County. There was one shut-off on Saturday night owing to the adjusting of the machinery, but since then the lights have been turned on without any further shut down. On Monday night, the lights were again turned on and burned a bright, white light fully up to the standard. The light burned steadily long after the stores closed for the night.*

In another related story, a reporter wrote, "The new hotel was lit up for the first time last night and presented a brilliant appearance, although only 98 of the 212 lights were used."

A companion story on the same page dealt with the sound of "heavy cannonading," which was "plainly heard in Fort Myers last Friday. It was the cruiser *Montgomery* practicing her guns at Boca Grande about 30 miles away down on air line. The firing was also heard at Marco fifty miles down the coast from Boca Grande."

That the small community was enthusiastic is reflected in another story three weeks later in which the *Press* reported, "Fort Myers To Have The Best." The story dealt with Gardner's decision to order a complete new plant so that there would be no interruption in service. "The new outfit will include a fifty horse power boiler and a 640 light dynamo…The two plants are to be connected in such a manner that no matter if one engine, boiler, or dynamo should give out, the other could be started up at once."

The *Press* quoted the cost of the plant at $6,000 and concluded in the same news story on the front page, "It is hardly necessary for us to say that Mr. Gardner deserves the most liberal support and encouragement in this important enterprise which adds so much to our town, and it would be but little for each citizen to stretch a point in standing by men who are willing to use their capital for the public good."

Grismer lends further light to life in Fort Myers during those early years when he writes, "All night service was provided only for the hotel. For all other customers, the current was shut off promptly at 11 p.m. Old timers recall that the lights in their homes always blinked several times exactly at 10:45. That was a signal the lights would go off fifteen minutes later." The electric bill paid by those first residential customers was thirty-five cents a week.

He adds, "The first ten street lights paid for by the town were installed along First Street from the hotel," which incidentally was first known as the Fort Myers Hotel and later as the Royal Palm Hotel.

These were exciting days. For the first time, people could walk down the town's main thoroughfare after dark without carrying lanterns.

Useppa
Home to Pirates and the Privileged
1895

T he sounds are the same...the rush of the winds through the crimped boughs of a live oak, the fingers of a breeze fondling the fronds of Areca and Washingtonia palms, the insistent searching of the lapping tongues of the tides as they play with the white, sandy shore.

But, wait! Are those voices of lusty Spanish seamen whose galleons once sailed these waters? Is that the sound of a young woman's keening wail, or the war cry of an enraged Caloosa determined to protect his lands from the greedy clutch of the white man? Is that the idle and relaxed laughter of the indolent and indulged, the upper class of our society?

No, of course not. These sounds can't be heard today, yet they ricochet through those corridors of memory labeled Useppa Island, corridors that stretch backward thousands of years.

The Caloosa Indians

Long before the life and death of the "Man from Galilee," Useppa is believed to have been known as the Island of Toempe and, as such, was the largest village of the Caloosa Indians. According to the American archaeologist Frank H. Cushing, who explored this area in 1895, the Caloosas were

The original Useppa Inn played host to presidents, inventors, movie stars and European royalty in its heyday. *Photo from the author's collection.*

people of the sea and lived along the shore in thatched huts fixed onto thick pilings firmly embedded in the sea bottom. The main feature of the village, however, was a large mound composed of shell and marl built up above the huts lining the water's edge. On this, which was used as a foundation, huts were built from palmetto fronds. The dwelling place of the chief was situated on the peak of the mound.

Cushing is convinced that the Caloosas were excellent engineers and that these mounds were designed and constructed to serve definite functions. They were not, as is often thought, just refuse piles. The Indians themselves have been described as being copper-skinned, of medium height, heavy in build with long, black hair they wore tied back from their faces. Their diet consisted largely of fish—mullet, mullet roe, mackerel, sheepshead and grouper, among others—along with deer, turkey, quail, berries, fruit and sea grapes.

Nearby Demere Key was believed to have been the site of a temple with altars at various elevations where the Caloosas came by canoe to worship. According to research done by author Florence Fritz for her book *The Unknown Story of World Famous Sanibel and Captiva*, the Caloosa Indians treated their deceased with deference, building burial mounds of sand for the remains.

Archaeologists and geologists have determined that this section of Florida was peopled by the Caloosas as early as 500 BC. Scant data is available concerning the interim years, but history records the fact that they were still here in 1513 when Ponce de Leon first sailed to Florida. According to Fritz's first book, *Unknown Florida,* maps from de Leon's expedition indicate that the Spanish explorer sailed into Charlotte Harbor and Pine Island Sound.

Beginning with Ponce de Leon's arrival, the Caloosa region was marked by strife and battle involving several would-be conquerors, including Panfilo de Narvaez (1529) and Hernando de Soto (1539). The next attempt worthy of note was undertaken in 1566 when Hernando Menendez de Aviles sailed from St. Augustine, which he had founded in 1565. From then until his death in 1574, Menendez tried by various methods to conquer the Caloosas—none of which was successful. Menendez, however, did have eighteen Caloosa chiefs and their great chief, Carlos, beheaded.

The Indians received further setbacks in the years ahead, although they fought bitterly and ferociously to retain supremacy in their land. In the early 1700s, slavery became an additional threat. A slave route was established by the Spanish between the area of Lake Okeechobee and the territories of Georgia and South Carolina. Then, about ten years later, the Spanish governor ordered all the remaining Caloosas transported and exiled to the heartland of the state.

The next blow fell in 1763 when Spain traded Florida to Great Britain in exchange for Cuba. Many of the Indians and Spanish-Indians who had been converted to Catholicism left Florida and migrated to Santo Domingo. Finally, twenty years later, further confusion resulted when Spain again acquired Florida after lengthy negotiations with England.

By this time, as a result of the sporadic warring over a period spanning 270 years and the cultural and biological influences from other races, the ancient Caloosa tribe was virtually extinct.

THE PIRATES

However, an equally intriguing if questionable chapter in Useppa's history had begun the preceding year when local lore has it that an admiral in the Spanish navy had been found guilty of attempting to steal the crown jewels.

The admiral, Jose Gaspar, escaped from Spanish authorities, seized one of the navy's finest ships and sailed from Spain to Florida. He sailed into Charlotte Harbor and made Gasparilla Island the headquarters for his new profession: piracy.

There is no question that pirates did exist in those turbulent years. Nor is there any question that they used Charlotte Harbor and Pine Island Sound as a base from which to operate. Historians have found naval documents that confirm this. As for Pine Island Sound, it was ideal for three reasons. The deep water accommodated the large ships. The many islands permitted the pirates, who used secret channels, to play hide-and-go-seek with their pursuers. The tall Caloosa Indian mounds provided an excellent vantage point with panoramic views of the surrounding waters.

[The existence of Jose Gaspar is still in question. He is largely believed to have been a figment of the fertile imagination of Barron Collier from New York, who made his fortune in advertising. Collier bought Useppa in 1912 and launched an ad campaign featuring Gaspar. On the other hand, it has not been disproved either. If the stories and legends are to be accepted, then he did have considerable impact on Useppa.]

After establishing himself as a pirate, Gaspar, or Gasparilla as he became known, reportedly lived on Gasparilla Island and used Useppa as one of the hiding places for his treasure. As was the wont of pirates in those long ago days, Gasparilla was reputed to have taken many women captives and to have kept them on a neighboring island, Captiva. Those from wealthy families he held for ransom. The others he used until he became bored and then executed them.

In 1801 Gasparilla met his romantic match and eventually made Useppa Island the repository for one of his most cherished treasures.

As the story goes, Gasparilla captured a Spanish ship en route from Mexico forty miles offshore from Boca Grande. He confiscated the ship's cache of gold and its more precious cargo—twelve young Mexican girls and personal maids. They were traveling to Spain to be educated. One of the girls, the youngest daughter of a viceroy of Mexico, caught Gasparilla's eye and heart. According to author Jack Beater, who wrote *Tales of South Florida and the 10,000 Islands*, the girl was identified as Josefa de Mayorga.

She was a beauty: young—about sixteen years old—and as arrogant and independent as Gasparilla. The hardhearted buccaneer became obsessed with her and at last, for safekeeping, he imprisoned her on what came to be known as Josefa's Island. (Later the name was corrupted into Useppa by local fishermen.) There he kept her under armed guard and would visit her as often as time and his "business" activities would permit. Patient at first, he treated her with respect and courtesy, but the girl, distraught with anger and yearning for her family and home, would have nothing to do with him. At last, in a fit of rage, he is reported to have had her decapitated while he watched. He had her buried on the island in an unmarked grave.

The ghost of the fierce and tormented Josefa haunted Gasparilla until his self-inflicted death in 1821. By that time, the United States government had cracked down on pirates. Sensing the end was near, Gasparilla divided $30 million in loot among his lieutenants. He was preparing to sail to some unknown haven when what seemed to be an English merchant ship appeared in the Gulf. The temptation was too strong and Gasparilla readied for the attack. As he did so, the ship dropped her disguise and showed her true colors. She was an American man-of-war and armed for battle. Defeated in the brief battle that followed, Gasparilla supposedly wound a length of anchor chain around his waist and jumped overboard.

There is an interesting postscript to this story contained in Elinor Dormer's intriguing book *The Seashell Islands*. She mentions that John Gomez had drawn a map showing the location of Josefa's grave before his death in 1900 at Panther Key. (Gomez was one of the sources of the tales of Gasparilla's exploits and claimed to be his brother-in-law.) The map was followed and, according to Dormer, the skeleton of a headless woman was found where Gomez had indicated.

THE FISHERMEN

Dormer also has another version of the origin of the island's name. According to her theory, Jose Caldez, a fisherman, used the island as a camp in the early 1800s. It was called Josefa, the feminine form of Jose, which was also reportedly the name of Caldez's boat. However, the name Josefa was changed to Guiseppa in 1870 when an Italian fisherman living on the island gave the census taker the revised form. Later, American homesteaders corrupted the island's name by shortening it to Useppa.

Written records are somewhat scarce for the years that follow, but historians have documented that in 1821, the United States purchased Florida from Spain for $5 million. Prior to this purchase, Spanish fishermen had established camps on the islands in the Pine Island Sound and were enjoying a prosperous life catching and selling fish to Cuba. By 1831, four fishing camps were in business in the area and customs collector William A. Whitehead was ordered to the camps to report on whether or not these fishermen were affecting the livelihoods of the American settlers there.

To this end, Whitehead, in company with the captain of the revenue cutter *Marion*, visited Pine Island and Useppa in late November 1831. According to Whitehead's notes, they found the first fishing camp on the north end of Pine Island deserted and assumed everyone was fishing. After spending the night onboard the *Marion*, they arrived at Useppa early the next morning and were met and welcomed by Jose Caldez, who had known Whitehead previously.

Caldez fixed them a breakfast consisting of fish, potatoes, onions, bread and coffee. Whitehead and the crew of the *Marion* stayed only a short period of time before traveling on to the other fishing camps. After his return to Key West, Whitehead reported to his superiors that the Spanish fishermen were not infringing upon the Americans.

In spite of his report, a licensing law was passed that required that the Spanish fishermen pay a license fee of $500 a year and Dr. Henry B. Crews was appointed to collect the monies and enforce the law. Dr. Crews and his wife moved onto Useppa and were living there in late 1835 when the Second Seminole War began.

In fact, the Crewses were still living on Useppa and Jose Caldez was still operating a fishing camp there in April 1836 when twenty-five Seminoles led by Chief Wyhokee attacked. Both sites were burned and looted. According to Dormer, the Spanish fishermen fled, returning to their homes only after the commander of the USS *Vandalia* had ascertained that the marauders were gone. At the time of the raid, Mrs. Crews was in Key West and Dr. Crews was hunting. His body, along with those of his crew, was found in a badly mutilated condition at the mouth of the Caloosahatchee River. This led the Spanish and the Spanish-Indians to leave the area, going to a fishery in Tampa Bay where they could work with less fear of attack by the Seminoles.

In 1845, Florida became the twenty-seventh state of the Union and Monroe County, which included what is today known as Lee County, was formed. The Spanish fishermen continued to fish the waters of Charlotte Harbor and San Carlos Bay until the 1880s, but no information is available of any activity on Useppa until the Gay Nineties. Then the island was purchased by John M. Roach, a streetcar magnate from Chicago.

THE AFFLUENT AND THE FAMOUS

According to *The Legend of Useppa* by John Law Kerr, Roach had been wintering in Fort Myers. He would travel by train to Punta Gorda and from there, by steamer down the waters of Charlotte Harbor and San Carlos Bay then up the Caloosahatchee to Fort Myers. On these trips, he passed Useppa and became so fascinated with the beauty of the island and its elevation that in 1894 he bought it as a winter home for his family. In fact, he built a small cottage on the site of the present golf club and there ensconced his younger brother to supervise the construction of this winter home.

In his book, Kerr relates an authentic treasure tale that would seem to corroborate the tales of buried pirate gold on the island. Kerr says that as young Roach was sitting on the front porch of his cottage one evening, a schooner dropped anchor and two crewmen came ashore.

The men asked Roach if they might fill their water cask from a nearby spring on the shore about fifty yards south of the present number two tee on the golf course. They also asked if they might camp overnight on the island. Apparently, these requests were so commonplace coming from the crews of passing boats that Roach thought nothing of it and granted permission readily.

The next morning, he was surprised when he started to the spring for water to see that the schooner was already gone. He was even more surprised to find when he reached their campsite—about halfway to the spring—that the strangers had dug a large hole at the base of a nearby tree. At the bottom of this hole was the imprint of a box about the size of a seaman's chest. Thinking treasure had been unearthed, Roach grabbed his gun and was soon in pursuit. Despite the speed of his sharpie (a long, sharp, flat-bottomed boat with triangular sails), Roach failed to catch up with the thieves.

Later, in 1916, when the golf course was being built, the excavation—which had never been filled in—lay just to the left of the number two fairway and was maintained as a trap. According to Kerr, "As the greenskeeper was cleaning out the trap, he found a small octagonal gold Spanish coin, about the size of a dime." Kerr goes on to assume that this coin could only have come from the stolen chest taken from the hole and therefore verified that Useppa was once a "pirate rendezvous." Jack Beater in his book *Pirates and Buried Treasure* describes the coin as being designed with a two-headed eagle with crown and spears dated 1761.

Time passed. The Roach family winter home was completed. Tarpon fishing was now the rage and the waters off Useppa abounded with the spirited game fish.

Kerr describes what happened next.

> *Soon a man named Hews appeared in Captiva with an old scow on which he had arranged crude quarters for ten or twelve fishermen. Edward Vom Hoffe was fishing from the Hews boat when he took his famous 210 pound tarpon, which was the record fish for so many years. Vom Hoffe had such a desperate struggle with his old-fashioned leather thumb brake reel that he later invented his automatic handle dragreel that is now used for all large fish.*
>
> *Tarpon fishing in the passes grew so popular that the Hews boat could not accommodate the fishermen, who soon induced Mr. Roach to build a small Inn on Useppa for them.*

Useppa Inn was opened in 1902. A large frame building situated right on the shore, it had twenty guest rooms. Kerr says the inn was operated with varying degrees of success until 1912 when Kerr's nephew, Barron Collier of New York City, bought the island.

Also in 1912, the famous Izaak Walton Club of Useppa was founded by Collier. It was named to honor writer Izaak Walton, who penned the classic *The Compleat Angler*. Kerr says it was soon recognized as the leading club in America and its buttons were most highly prized. The buttons were awarded to tarpon fishers only. The first tarpon caught netted one a silver button, a 100-pound tarpon merited a gold button and a tarpon weighing 150 pounds brought the fortunate fisherman a diamond button. The Izaak Walton Club was responsible for beginning the practice of releasing tarpon, with the exception of those that had to be weighed for the awarding of buttons.

In future years, Useppa became an internationally known and exclusive tarpon fishing resort. Sportsmen from Europe journeyed to the remote island each season. Members from our country's wealthiest and most prestigious families—the Mellons, the du Ponts, the Rothschilds—fished there along with Presidents Theodore Roosevelt and Herbert Hoover. Luminaries from Hollywood including Shirley Temple, Hedy Lamarr, Mae West, Gloria Swanson, World Heavyweight Champion Gene Tunney and writer Zane Grey visited. Their signatures are visible today on the discolored pages of the inn's registers.

While Collier owned Useppa, he made wide-ranging improvements. He constructed a number of frame guest bungalows as well as a three-story mansion for himself and his family. He also built the nine-hole golf course that gave golfers the unique opportunity of teeing off for the fourth hole from the deck of a schooner dubbed the *Boat Tee*. Collier installed a swimming pool, tennis courts, an airstrip and even an illegal gambling casino, which Mary Roberts Rinehart has written of in her books. Rinehart lived in a cottage on Useppa for two or three years before moving to Cabbage Key.

THE INVADERS

By the 1950s, the resort was no longer the fashionable vacation spot it had once been—business was slow and got even slower. However, Useppa came to life once more in April of 1960. Again it was the scene of war-inspired maneuvers, but this time as a training ground.

The episode began in Miami when a Lee County attorney, William Lamar Rose, who has since served as circuit court judge here, was approached.

Judge Rose says, "My hunting camp in the Everglades was being used to train about three thousand Cuban counterrevolutionaries who had been recruited to take part in the Bay of Pigs invasion. I was trying a case in federal court when one of the attorneys for the Justice Department came up to me and asked if I knew where there was an island with deep water around it. I told him Useppa."

Judge Rose, for the time being, heard no more about the request. However, his information had been taken very seriously. Former Sheriff Flanders "Snag" Thompson picks up the tale.

> *It was top secret. I had a contact with the CIA and I was to let him know if anything happened on the island. That person had a code name, at least I assume it was, and a phone number in Tampa that I was to call if anything happened.*
>
> *They were training some of the officers and the soldiers there. They flew the men in by planes. One group of around a hundred men would fly in and stay for about ten days training, then they would be taken out and another group flown in. They were there about sixty days all told.*

The cottages Collier had constructed as well as the Useppa Inn were put to a strange new use. Instead of housing wealthy and renowned vacationers, they housed would-be soldiers. And the grounds that had been outfitted with appurtenances for leisurely recreation were now the scene of war games, killing strategy and survival techniques. The atmosphere that had been relaxed, indolent, casual was now fierce and intense.

"The supplies and groceries were brought down by truck from Tampa to Boca Grande," Thompson continues. "My deputy on Boca Grande—Johns Knight—carried their supplies to them by boat. He was the only one who ever had contact with them and that was very brief. They would unload the boat at the docks and that's as far as he was allowed to go."

An armed guard was on duty patrolling the island around the clock. Thompson feels sure the area fishermen knew they were there—the soldiers could be seen from passing boats. However, the sheriff says he only had one inquiry and that was from two local businessmen who were out fishing one weekend. They approached the island, but were not allowed to land. When they asked him about it, Thompson says, "I just gave them an excuse and that was it." And so it was that one of Useppa's most colorful, though brief, chapters concluded in almost total secrecy.

Useppa was silent once more. The palmettos, scrub oaks and native grasses reached out to reclaim the island. The tangled web of tropical growth obscured the white beach Barron Collier had so carefully created with imported sand. Useppa slumbered. And waited. Waited for the next chapter in its intriguing, compelling chronology.

THE MODERNS

Then in 1973 Mariner Properties, the owners and managers of South Seas Plantation on Captiva, bought Useppa for approximately $1.4 million. Still Useppa dozed until 1977, when Garfield R. Beckstead created the Useppa Inn and Dock Company, and, in partnership with Mariner Properties, began restoring the island and its facilities.

Beckstead and his crew restored the Barron Collier residence, now used as an inn, along with its lounge, game rooms, party rooms and a museum room, which has on display the original guest registers and memorabilia from Collier's Izaak Walton Tarpon Club. The walls are replete with a mounted tarpon, tarnished silver loving cups and hanging baskets with striped spider plants. There's an old Wainwright piano, the wood lovingly polished to a sheen.

They've restored the general store, main clubhouse, the golf pro shop, the tennis courts and three holes of the golf course. All the major buildings have been restored. The original wood has been refinished and much of the wicker furniture is once again in service.

"We want to maintain and reconstruct the ambiance of the '20s," Beckstead says of this island retreat. And indeed it would follow that he also wishes to reestablish the exclusivity of the island's population. "Eighty-five individual home sites selected for elevation and view have been planned for eventual development and sale to club members," reads the brochure. The lots sell for between $50,000 and $70,000 and only 25 percent remained unsold in the fall of 1978, according to their fact sheet.

In a determined effort to preserve the island's atmosphere, deed restrictions require architecture to be consistent with that of the 1920s. Furthermore, the home sites have been selected to provide a view, but also to protect the island's foliage.

The club referred to in the fact sheet is the Useppa Island Club and was started by Beckstead. There are two types of memberships. Permanent life guarantees individual families access to the island and its facilities. The second is group membership for business and professional affiliates, which entitles them to use the island and its facilities for small groups of not more than fifteen people. In addition, club membership permits one to purchase a home site with the cost of the membership—$1,500—deducted from the cost of the land. At this writing, membership has been restricted to five hundred, but provision has been made to increase this number if the majority of existing members concur.

The sounds of hammers and saws and television sets now pervade Useppa's environs, but these are the only changes, other than flurries of activity at various times around the general store and the inn. Yes, several new homes have been built, but they are by no means obtrusive. John Roach and Barron Collier would probably feel quite at home. Useppa is still beautiful, still fascinating whether you pass by in a boat or have the privilege of following Collier's pink concrete promenade across her historic mounds and shores.

Originally published in the March 1979 issue of *Lee Living*.

THE BOULEVARD PAVED WITH BONES
1913

Take heart if in the season of ghouls and specters, it should happen that one night as you travel McGregor Boulevard you encounter a ghastly column of skeletons stumbling en masse toward an unknown destination. In the seventy-seven years since these skeletons were first quite literally excavated, they've never been known to harm a living soul. Yet they represent one of the most intriguing mysteries of this area's history.

The year was 1913, the month September. The country was fascinated by the sensational murder of wealthy New York architect Stanford White by Harry K. Thaw. The murderer—he shot White in front of many witnesses on the roof of Madison Square Garden—had fled to Canada, where he had been captured, and the issue of his extradition was headline news.

Locally, discussion centered on building Lee County's first hospital on Victoria Avenue. A $47,000 bond issue had been approved to build a yellow brick $35,000 high school on Thompson Street in Fort Myers, and a $10,000 school in LaBelle. (LaBelle was in Lee County because Hendry County had not yet been formed.) Tempers had matched the summer's heat and were only now cooling down in the aftermath of the defeat of a proposed $200,000 bond issue to build roads detoured by a vote of 272 to 249.

Much like today, roads were a popular, emotion-ridden topic of discussion, and not just because of the road bond issue. Growth, also much

In this 1913 photo taken by project engineer Maurice A. Pearl, a construction worker sat on one of the cars used to transport the shell (and bones) from Sword Point to a boat, which then carried the material to the mainland. *Courtesy of Robert Pearl.*

as today, was a factor. Lee County's population had nearly quadrupled in two decades, exploding from 1,414 in 1890 to 6,294 in 1910. Civic and business leaders were actively promoting growth and they saw paved streets and roads as an absolute necessity.

Mrs. Tootie McGregor Terry, widow of Ambrose M. McGregor, a major stockholder in Standard Oil, before she remarried Dr. Marshall Orlando Terry, former U.S. surgeon general and one of the six wealthiest men in the nation, had long been a winter resident and staunch booster of Fort Myers and Lee County. In 1912 she had offered to build, at her expense, a fifty-foot-wide boulevard from Punta Rassa to Whiskey Creek. There were two stipulations: first, that the city and county continue the boulevard from Whiskey Creek to Monroe Street in downtown Fort Myers and second, that the boulevard be named to honor her first husband. With alacrity, both the Fort Myers City Council and the Lee County Commission had approved the project and that section from Punta Rassa to Whiskey Creek was now under construction.

Maurice A. Pearl, who'd come here in 1912 from Michigan, was the construction engineer in charge of the project. He and his crew were excavating oyster shells to use on the road from Sword Point, a small island at the mouth of the Caloosahatchee River and San Carlos Bay.

According to the September 24 edition of the *Fort Myers Daily Press*, the discovery of the burial ground occurred approximately ten days earlier. It had to have been a harrowing experience for the construction crewmember when his shovel uncovered a skull that rolled down the slight grade to rest at his feet. What was even more harrowing was that by the end of that first day they had unearthed fifty-seven skeletons.

As the road crew continued work, they ultimately exhumed a total of 103 skeletons. The only other item unearthed was a broken, unglazed piece of pottery.

According to Pearl as recounted in the *Daily Press*, "No regularity whatever has been followed in the disposition of the bodies in the ridge. Some lie flat on the face; others prone on the back. Some have arms extended; some bodies are at right angles to each other; some are piled in a heap, while one, as previously related in the *Press*, is holding a broken bowl of unglazed pottery."

Pearl was further quoted in the same article as theorizing that the skeletons were those of "persons of ordinary size. The teeth remaining in a few of the jaws lead to the conclusion that some of the individuals were very young men, while other mouth cavities are worn so smooth that it is believed very old men must have been in the party."

Dr. W.P. Winkler, local physician and surgeon, had recently opened his practice on First Street in the Bradford block. Already well regarded in town, he was apparently the closest to a forensic pathologist the area had and several of the skeletons were taken to him for study. While he did not propose a theory as to why the 103 human beings had died, he concluded in the *Press* that the skeletons were "those of white persons. The profile is straight, and the cheek bones do not seem to be high enough for those of Indians."

Several theories were put forward. Captain F.A. Hendry, regarded locally as the area's foremost historian since he was a local pioneer and had been on the scene to witness the discovery, felt the bones dated prior to the Seminole Indian Wars.

In an article that appeared in the *Press* a few weeks later on October 2, Dr. A.E. Phillips of Sanford, Florida, the author of a book titled *The Romance of The Ten Thousand Islands*, theorized that the bodies were those of pirates killed in an engagement with a U.S. gunboat assigned to the area by the navy to suppress piracy in the Gulf of Mexico.

Phillips wrote the newspaper and said, "I am reminded of a fight between the U.S. Marines and a gang of pirates occurring on one of the little islands off the coast of west Florida in which the pirates were exterminated and their bodies buried in a mound. Of course there were no arms or implements interred with them. The bones and skulls found at this day in a mound…are perhaps those of these very criminals."

Pearl was careful to document his find with photographs that were developed by F.W. Hunt, a well-known Fort Myers photographer. Pearl then went one step further. He sent some of the skulls and bones to the Smithsonian Institute for study and evaluation.

Robert Pearl of north Fort Myers says that the family lost track of Maurice Pearl and does not know what happened to the photographs and other documents. In an interesting twist, Robert Pearl, who has lived in Lee County most of his life, learned of the skeletons when a cousin sent him an old clipping from the *Palladium*, a newspaper published in Benton Harbor, Michigan.

And what happened to the rest of the skeletons? The majority of the bones were so old and fragile they shattered while being excavated. Since they could not be separated, they were included in the shell used to pave that section of McGregor Boulevard extending from Punta Rassa to Whiskey Creek.

So, if in this Halloween season of spirits you travel the beautiful boulevard paved with the broken bones of those early pioneers, don't be frightened. Even if you encounter this ghastly group of unknowns who rest not in consecrated ground, remember: in the seventy-seven years since they were exposed, they've yet to surface—other than as a boulevard.

Originally published in the September–October 1992 issue of *Lee Living*.

THE NIGHT
THEY TORE THE
COURTHOUSE DOWN
1914

The year was 1914. The civilized world was embroiled in World War I. The *Fort Myers Press*'s headlines screamed, "Over 4,500,000 Troops Now Battling on the East Prussian Border…Cholera Raging in the Austrian Army."

Meanwhile, things weren't all that peaceful in Fort Myers. True, there was no bloodshed and the armies were miniscule in terms of manpower, but both sides were vocal and determined.

The controversy centered on the county courthouse. On one side were the proponents for a new, modern, three-story concrete courthouse. This group was led by "Wild" Bill Towles, who was both president of the Fort Myers City Council and chairman of the Lee County Board of Commissioners. In this instance, he was supported by the *Press*, which labeled the frame courthouse "unsightly and unsanitary," claiming it marred the horizon.

Towles was opposed by Harvie Heitman, a very thrifty, successful businessman. In all fairness, it must be pointed out that Heitman was not against progress per se. Indeed, his $85,000 Earnhardt Building on Hendry Street was under construction that summer. When first built, the building boasted the only public bathroom in town, complete with hot and cold running water.

On the other hand, Towles had wanted and worked for a courthouse that would adequately represent Lee County as the prosperous and progressive

The original frame Lee County Courthouse. *Courtesy of the Southwest Florida Historical Museum.*

area he truly felt it was. His drive for a new courthouse had begun in 1887, shortly after Lee County was formed.

According to Karl Grismer in his history of Fort Myers, "By working tirelessly, he [Towles] managed to win enough support to get a $30,000 bond issue approved by a 100 to 47 vote. But then the hard times of the early '90s came along, the bonds could not be sold, and finally Lee County had to be satisfied with a piddling wooden courthouse which cost only $3,640."

But now economic times were better, the frame courthouse was twenty years old and Towles felt he had waited long enough.

Local attorney J. Franklin Garner, who has researched the legal documents, recalls that Towles still had many obstacles to overcome. "The first time Mr. Harvie Heitman and his group got an injunction in Circuit Court," Garner said, "the first time it was because the county had failed to pass a resolution of the necessity of building a courthouse. So they threw the bond issue out and the contract was cancelled." This was early in 1914.

In August of that year, ads signed by Towles as chairman of the county commissioners and H.A. Hendry as county clerk appeared in the *Press* calling for bids to construct a courthouse according to plans and specifications prepared by F.J. Kennard, an architect from Tampa.

An article appearing in the following Tuesday's paper said merely that G.A. Miller of Tampa had been the successful bidder, but he "was not ready to sign the contract, which will be ready for his acceptance at the regular meeting of the board at their meeting in October."

The article went on to say that the opposition had served notices and filed a bill to "enjoin the commissioners from erecting the courthouse."

The first bid had been for $74,900. Miller's bid, according to Garner, was around $80,000. And, according to Garner, "The second time that they awarded the contract, and after the contract was awarded, they tied the interest onto it for building the courthouse, which was illegal. So he [Towles] was out again."

However, Towles was a determined and persistent man. Another ad calling for bids to build the courthouse appeared in the *Press* in early October. Bids were to be opened at "twelve o'clock noon on the 24th day of October 1914." And on the front page of that afternoon's paper there appeared an article stating that F.P. Heifner, a contractor from Atlanta, had been awarded the contract. His low bid was $100,000.

However, the opposition was equally determined and in the paragraph following the information concerning the awarding of the bid, the article reported that notice of an application for an injunction had been filed. The applicants were D.S. Borland, a citrus grower, and C.L. Johnson and John Dyler, attorneys.

Garner, who was in the second or third grade here at the time, tells the story. "They [the commissioners] had a quick meeting and passed a resolution authorizing Towles to proceed to build the courthouse in any way he saw fit. They gave him complete authority. So he got together with the contractor in a little meeting and, as I recall, it was the early part of the afternoon. Maybe around 2:30 or 3 o'clock."

Garner was born and grew up in the home that forms that section of the Veranda Restaurant fronting on Second Street. At the time, according to city maps, Broadway was called Garrett Street and it did not go through to First Street, but ended at Main Street. Garner had a front-row seat for the events about to unfold.

I saw this group of men coming down Second Street from the east. It looked to me at that time like it was about a mob of one hundred or so. All of them had things in their hands like an ax or crowbar or some kind of tool.

And Towles was walking at the head of them right down the middle of the street.

They turned the corner on Garrett and went down to the courthouse. Part of the men went up on the roof and started knocking off shingles. The other part of them went into the building and started hauling out furniture and all of the records and books.

Garner remembers that Towles was sitting out in front of the building watching the proceedings. Grismer writes, "Old timers say Towles sat on steps nearby with a shot gun in his hands, ready to take a pot shot at anyone who tried to halt the demolition job."

"The train station was over where the Lee County Bank is today," Garner continues. "And Mr. Francis W. Perry and Mr. C.L. Johnson, the two attorneys, got on the train to go to Arcadia to get the injunction and that's when the work started in earnest.

"Then when it got dark, they took all the broken boards and shingles off the roof and they had bonfires around the building so they could see."

Garner watched their progress through the night from the sleeping porch of his family's home. "When the sun came up the next morning, all of the lumber that was any good was stacked in piles and nobody was there. It got daylight and there was one little room standing there. I guess that was where the vault or safe was and that was the only thing standing," he says.

The lumber was put to good use. Garner says some of the people in town were incensed over the courthouse's destruction so to assuage them, Towles arranged to have the lumber from the courthouse given to the hospital that was proposed to be built at the corner of Grand and Victoria Avenues.

However, this was not the end of the feud. In the November 2, 1914 edition of the *Fort Myers Press*, Perry wrote an impassioned article headlined "The Opposition's Side of the Courthouse Controversy" in which he said, "the best elements of our society, the element which believes in the dignity and sanctity of the Courts, which does not believe in anarchy, but, willing to arbitrate its differences before the courts even though their decisions may compel silent and sometimes humiliating acquiescence ought to hang their head in shame when it contemplates the needless destruction of valuable property by its public officers."

On November 25, Judge F.A. Whitney ruled against Heitman and his group, denying the injunction, and on December 1, the *Press* reported, "The first carload of material...is on the way from the quarry in Georgia." On December 22, the *Press* reported that work had begun. They next reported that actual construction of the courthouse had begun.

The yellow brick courthouse that replaced the frame courthouse in 1914 is still in use ninety-two years later—a good investment. *Photo from the author's collection.*

In January 1915, the Board of County Commissioners, which had included Towles of Fort Myers, R.B. Collier of Estero, Edward Parkinson from Alva, Captain H.A. Hendry from LaBelle and Dr. W.S. Turner from Captiva, went out of office. However, the issue was not legally resolved until February 10 when the paper reported that Judge Whitney's decision had been sustained by the Florida Supreme Court and, in the same issue, reported that the new commissioners were refusing to pay the amount claimed due the contractor for work on the courthouse.

That dispute was resolved and on April 9, 1915, the *Press* announced that the cornerstone of the new yellow brick courthouse would be laid on April 13.

The entire town of Fort Myers turned out for the ceremony. The *Press* described the cornerstone as "marble upon which has been carved the names of the board of commissioners in office at the time the contract was made, the clerk of the court, contractor and architect."

The local Masonic Lodge, Tropical Lodge No. 56 F&AM, was in charge of "ritualistic ceremonies," in which they used corn, the symbol of plenty; wine, the symbol of refreshment and gladness; and oil, the emblem of peace and joy, applying these to the cornerstone. The ladies of the Eastern Star provided the music.

A lead box was sealed in the cornerstone. In it had been placed a number of items, including a copy of the *Press*, coins of various denominations, a copy of the plans and specifications of the courthouse, an old Bible, which under law since repealed was kissed by all jurors and witnesses, a copy of the minutes of the meeting of the first Board of Commissioners of Lee County held in 1888, a certified copy of the deed of Jane L. and Charles W. Hendry to the courthouse square and an inscribed Masonic apron and trowel.

Those ceremonies didn't mark the end of Garner's ties to the courthouse, for his father, James Franklin Garner Sr., was clerk of court from 1916 until 1932. And when English sparrows began nesting around the light globes at the new courthouse shortly after it was complete, Garner was pressed into service.

"When they turned the lights on, the nests would catch fire and those big globes would explode. You couldn't do it now," Garner said with a chuckle, "but they told me I could shoot the English sparrows in the courtyard and they bought these little shot shells for my .22 rifle—a thousand at a time. I spent my afternoons and out-of-school time shooting sparrows in the courtyard."

Today, the yellow brick courthouse stands in the shadow of the more modern addition completed in the late 1960s and the monolithic Justice Center but, in its time, it represented both progress and a hard-won victory for the pioneer citizens of what was then a frontier town.

Originally published in "Only Yesterday" in the *Fort Myers News-Press* on July 8, 1984.

Children of a Cult
1920

For nearly a century, the Koreshan Unity has been located in Estero. During those years, hundreds of thousands of words have been written about Cyrus Teed, the charismatic leader who formed the group, as well as his controversial theory that we live on the inside of the earth.

Much has also been written about the wealth of botanical and horticultural information harvested from Koreshan experiments and gardens. A modicum of material has even been generated concerning the Koreshans themselves, those hardy pioneers who turned over everything they owned to the Koreshan Unity and journeyed into the wilds of southwest Florida to live life according to Koresh (the Hebrew word for Cyrus). But what of the youngsters? What kind of life did the children of Koreshan Unity live?

Keep in mind that the last member of the Koreshan Unity died years ago. Keep in mind, too, that according to newspaper and first-person accounts, runaways were quite commonplace. The children of Koreshan Unity, those few still surviving, are spread throughout the country. Only two remain in southwest Florida: Irene Wyka Holtsclaw, seventy-eight, and her sister Naomi Wyka Whitaker, seventy-five. While Mrs. Whitaker was not feeling well enough for an interview, Mrs. Holtsclaw remembers well and, in fact, cherishes her years as a child at the Koreshan Unity.

This photo was taken when the Wyka children first arrived in the Koreshan Unity in Estero. The two older boys, Doug and Alex, are in the back row. In the front row are Eugene, Naomi (seated) and Irene. *Courtesy of Irene Holtsclaw.*

The five Wyka children—Irene Wyka Holtsclaw, her sister Naomi and their brothers Eugene, Alex and Douglas—arrived in Fort Myers in November of 1920. The train trip had been difficult, but no more difficult than the preceding year when their mother had died in St. Louis during childbirth. Their father, a tailor, had struggled to keep the family together, but had finally released the youngest child, Hazel, to a foster home and sent the other five to Florida.

One of Mrs. Holtsclaw's earliest memories is of that first night when they were met in Fort Myers by Sister Emily Bessemer and Brother Alfred

Christianson (members of the Unity addressed one another as "Sister" and "Brother"), who had driven from Estero to pick them up. Sister Emily had brought a treat for the children—a thermos of warm milk. Unfortunately, none of the children liked warm milk so it was more of a treatment than a treat.

The Koreshans believed in and practiced celibacy, so men and women lived separate lives. Not only were the sleeping arrangements separate, they were also segregated at meals in the dining hall. That first night when they arrived, the boys and girls were immediately split. The boys were sent to Amity House, a home on the grounds where the men lived, and the girls were housed in a room on the second floor over the dining hall.

The next morning when eight-year-old Irene Holtsclaw awoke, she formed a first impression of the Koreshan Unity that was to last to this day. "I walked across the room to the window which overlooked the beautiful gardens and saw the beautiful grapefruit trees loaded with fruit. Coming from St. Louis in the winter, which was so dreary and gray, I thought this must be heaven."

She soon learned that even in heaven there were rules and hard work to be done. But even before that, disaster struck. She had gotten lice on the long train trip. Sister Emily took her to the barber. Her long hair, her prize and delight, had to be shorn and her head washed with kerosene. She was given a white cap to wear, but while it covered her scalp it was no shield against her humiliation.

One of her first jobs was in the dining hall. Every morning she'd report downstairs, where she served breakfast. Tables were numbered and assigned according to rank and Mrs. Holtsclaw remembers the tables were properly appointed with crisp linen tablecloths and napkins that were changed and washed weekly.

The leaders were served first and their tables were numbered "one"—one for the male leaders, one for the female leaders. She served both number one tables, which was an honor. After the others were served, the children were permitted to eat. Following breakfast, they cleared the tables, washed and dried the dishes, swept the floors and attended school.

Classes were conducted by Sister Josephine Lester, a teacher from Nevada, from 8:30 until 11:30 a.m. The school was a room over the bakery and the students numbered between twenty-five and thirty. Sister Josephine taught her charges reading, writing, arithmetic, spelling, civics, history, grammar—all the traditional subjects. However, the curriculum was well rounded with an emphasis on music, art and drama. "You got personal attention," Mrs. Holtsclaw says today, "but you had to really work." She attended through the eighth grade, but feels it was the equivalent of a high school education.

Deportment and social graces were stressed, but the Koreshans believed in the sanctity of work and vocational training was considered essential. As a result, the children worked to learn a trade in the print shop, the bakery, the kitchen, the machine shop, boatyard, sawmill or one of the other Unity industries. The Koreshans were almost entirely self-sufficient so seldom had commerce with the outside world.

When Mrs. Holtsclaw was twelve or thirteen, she was assigned to work in the bakery. Every morning at 4:00 a.m., Brother George Hunt would call her from outside her window. She would dress and go down to the bakery, where she would help knead and bake the bread and rolls. The bakery was an important source of revenue, since the Koreshans sold baked goods in their store to "outsiders," which is what they called people who were not members of the Unity. Mrs. Holtsclaw also worked in the laundry and as a bearer or errand girl for Sister Etta Silverfreund.

Once the children had done the supper dishes, their time was their own. They could play games or cards. Extra library tables in the dining hall were loaded with books and magazines to read. Or they could go outside and play hide-and-go-seek. Trips to Fort Myers Beach were often organized. They could canoe on the Estero River, which ran through the Unity grounds. Three or four times a year, they would be taken to Fort Myers and at least once a year each child would be given a quarter to spend in the dime store as he or she saw fit.

It was not idyllic, however, and children sometimes ran away rather than adjust to the hard work and discipline—Mrs. Holtsclaw, as a Unity child, was often whipped for being sassy. In fact, her older brothers, Doug and Alex, ran away from the Unity and returned to St. Louis to be with their father. Naomi and Alex remained much longer, but Mrs. Holtsclaw eloped with an outsider when she was fifteen.

"It was a cult," Mrs. Holtsclaw says today. "They worshipped Teed and I never heard the word Jesus when I was there. But it was one of the best cults I've ever heard of…Teed was a man with a great dream. He wanted people to be better, to be the best they possibly could. And those people, they loved us. They were our family. They took care of us and loved us."

Readers can prove to themselves that we do indeed live in the center of the earth by consulting Cyrus Teed's "rectilineator." The rectilineator, which was the instrument that Teed invented to prove his theory, is on display in the Art Hall at the Koreshan State Park situated about fifteen miles south of Fort Myers on U.S. 41. The park is a fascinating place to spend either an afternoon or a weekend. Not only is the Koreshan State Park historic, it is beautiful as well.

On the Unity grounds, readers may enjoy the many exotic plants that Teed and his group brought from around the world in addition to plants and trees native to Florida. They'll see banks of bougainvilleas, stands of tall, agile bamboo, needle palms and the stately Washingtonia palm—to name but a few.

Originally published in the March–April 1991 edition of *Lee Living*.

A HAVEN FOR HISTORY
1924

The Seaboard Coastline (SCL) Railroad Station now houses the Southwest Florida Historical Museum at 2300 Peck Street. The terminal was the scene of a number of historic occasions in this area's history, including the arrival and departure of world-renowned inventor Thomas Edison when he wintered in Fort Myers. Presidents and movie stars and reporters debarked as well. Built in 1924 at a cost of close to $48,000, the train station bustled with activity and crowds for many years, especially in the autumn and spring when winter residents would arrive and depart. During World War II, it was the scene of many tearful farewells and reunions. In 1950, nearly the entire town—including the Fort Myers High School Band—crowded into the depot to give the local National Guard contingent a rousing send-off as the local boys went off to the Korean conflict.

As air travel, with its speed and convenience, became increasingly popular, railroads throughout the nation felt the pinch and Lee County was no exception. By 1971, with the advent of Amtrak (which bypassed Fort Myers), the SCL Railroad decided to close the depot here. The station became a haven for vagrants and winos. Winds and rains blew through its cloistered walkways and its broken windows.

There were, however, many citizens of Fort Myers who admired the beauty of the terminal—people who really wanted a historical museum

The train station, shown here shortly after its completion in 1924, today houses the Southwest Florida Historical Museum. *Courtesy of the Southwest Florida Historical Museum.*

where our heritage could be preserved—and they started to work, led by then-Mayor Oscar M. Corbin Jr.

A sixteen-acre tract housed the train yard and the depot, and it had become a blighted area in the heart of town with rapidly deteriorating buildings. Corbin felt it could and should be improved. In 1974, he negotiated for its purchase from the railroad for $806,900 and a firm was hired to prepare a conceptual utilization study. Their recommendations concurred with his convictions; namely, that the land would lend itself to redevelopment as a cultural site, while opening up the area from a traffic standpoint as well. As a result of his early efforts, the Lee County School Board purchased the site on which they have constructed their administration building. Furthermore, the new Fort Myers/Lee County Public Library was constructed adjacent to the museum.

The museum was by no means assured, even at this stage. In 1976 the roof was repaired, but in 1977, after Corbin left office, work was halted on the structure until May 1978. At that time, a contract was signed with H.D. Rutledge & Sons for $110,000 to repair the exterior walls and sand and finish the doors and windows. In 1979, another $26,000 was allocated to complete the renovation of the exterior and the cleaning of the interior. Five years had now passed. The renovation had been complete, but the building remained a shell, and city officials were reluctant to pour more tax dollars into the project.

At this point, private citizens took the lead in fundraising efforts. At the helm were Lloyd Hendry, a local attorney and descendant of pioneer Captain Francis Asbury Hendry; Lloyd's wife, Jody; and Mrs. Heard Edwards. They were joined by numerous other civic-minded residents.

In July 1980, a fundraising campaign was launched. The goal was to raise $400,000 to complete the restoration of the interior of the depot and to provide operating funds. The campaign was to last eleven weeks. By the middle of August, contributions had reached $406,000, and by the end of the drive in mid-September 1980, they totaled $430,000.

In addition to agreeing to underwrite the actual cost of the fundraising campaign, the City of Fort Myers entered into a contract with a paper-recycling company in Miami and residents were urged to save and donate their old newspapers. The city now receives approximately twenty-four dollars per ton for the newspapers, and this money is allocated for the operation of the museum.

By April 1981, the final phase of the renovation was begun, with the awarding of a contract to Nu-Cape Construction Company for the electrical work and the paving of the parking lot and sidewalks. In June 1981, the SCL Railroad donated two railroad cars, and in July, the museum's first director, Patti Bartlett, was hired. Then, in November, Mark Appleby was hired as a technician to assist her in the design and construction of exhibits.

Six years of hard work, of planning and of fundraising were finally rewarded on April 6, 1982, when the Fort Myers Historical Museum first opened its doors to the public. Today, it stands not only as a monument to the past, but also to the present; for it represents the people of Fort Myers who had a dream and a goal, and who persevered until they saw their dream come to life.

Originally published by the Metropolitan Fort Myers Chamber of Commerce in 1983.

Iona Schoolhouse
Once the Heart of Its Community
1924

Once the grounds of the Iona Schoolhouse echoed with the laughter and shouting of schoolchildren. Fishermen and farmers, the people of its community, held town meetings and dances and cakewalks in its classrooms.

After it was closed in the early 1950s, the red brick building was used to store gladiolus bulbs. And then it was purchased and used as a studio by an interior designer. Next it housed a firm of architects. Now it is home to an advertising firm, but construction is underway and soon the playgrounds will be the site of an office park.

Jeff Condon, president of Southwestern General Contractors and a Michigan transplant, bought the school and site from local designer Kappy King Cole in October of 1984. In August 1985, Condon began clearing the land. Last December he broke ground on two buildings totaling 9,500 square feet and says the Iona Schoolhouse Professional Center will be completed by the early part of May.

When finished, there will be a total of thirteen thousand square feet in the $800,000 complex and nine units, which will be both leased and offered as condos, Condon says. Seti Advertising has leased the original building and will remain. The new space will go for $12 a square foot.

According to Condon, the structure is being built with no interior partitions so it can be finished to meet the needs of the individual business, including plumbing and electrical. Size will range from 1,100 square feet on up.

The Iona Schoolhouse. *Photo from the author's collection.*

In explaining why he selected the building, Condon says, "We've been coming to Florida for fifteen years on Sanibel. When we moved to Fort Myers two years ago, we fell in love with that building."

This also explains why Condon and his architect, Bruce T. Gora, have gone to great lengths to retain the look of the original schoolhouse and even the grounds, saving more than forty palms and every live oak on the property.

"We are using three different types of brick to match the brick in the original building," he says. "All the windows in the new building are nine panes over nine panes to match the old ones. Even the stucco work will look old. We don't want the buildings to look as though someone just added them. It's designed to look as though it was one unit."

Architectural Resources, a local architectural firm, leased the building for seven years from Kappy King Cole, the interior designer who bought the building in the 1960s. Joe Barany of Architectural Resources says the building is "a fairly typical institutional building for its time…brick with wood framing for the roof as well as the floor. The floor was elevated over the crawl space. It is not particularly indigenous to Florida; it is more typical of Georgia, Alabama or the Florida panhandle."

Barany says he and the other architects especially liked the lintels, the beams spanning the windows and doors. "They were wood," he says. "Typically those are stone or concrete or steel. We considered this a fairly distinctive feature."

The building's charm captivated Barany and his firm tried to buy the school from Cole, but the timing was wrong. When they wanted to buy she wasn't ready to sell, and when she was ready they were already committed to another site.

The school's origins are shrouded in mystery. The first mention of the Iona School is in early 1924. In July 1924, the Board of Public Instruction (as it was known then) contracted to purchase the site from Dr. Franklin Miles for $500. Late that year, board members voted to sell $10,000 in school bonds.

They didn't accomplish that goal, however, and in 1926, the board, noting the original issue had not been sold, voted to sell $50,000 in a new bond issue. There the record ends. By late 1926, teachers' salaries at the school were duly noted in the school board minutes, but there is no record of the putting out for bids or awarding of the construction contract. There are no architectural specifications, no drawings, no information about the building, which officially, it would seem, was never built.

Longtime Iona resident George Watson remembers his years as a student there. He attended Iona Elementary from 1932 through 1939, grades one through seven.

"At that time, there was no electricity running down toward Punta Rassa," he says. "We did have lights in the building after somebody started the generator in the pavilion out back." But the school did have heaters in each classroom—large wood stoves. The school board hired a man to cut wood for the stoves, but the students carried it inside and kept the stoves going.

The school had three classrooms. Two opened into a large auditorium. The other was at the front of the building. There was no cafeteria and most of the pupils carried their lunches, but Watson remembers the school had a kitchen and sometimes the teachers would cook a big pot of soup there.

Watson's brother, Charles, now principal at Alva Middle School, attended Iona School from 1942 through 1949. And that big pot of soup plays an important role in his memories, for it apparently became a school tradition.

"On Wednesday mornings," Charles Watson recalls, "one of the older boys would ride a bicycle to Frank's store near Iona Loop Road and pick up a big, meaty soup bone Mr. Smothers would save for us. Then the older girls would make a big pot of beef vegetable soup and sell it for five cents a bowl. The money would be used to buy the ingredients for next week's soup."

And Charles Watson remembers the school played an important and often poignant role in the community.

Mrs. Evans, the principal, would have a play every big holiday…Christmas, Thanksgiving, Halloween, Easter. And every student in the school would be incorporated in that production in some way. Every kid would be seen. And all the parents would come to the school to see their kids.

This was during the war years, remember, and every time a boy from the community was home on leave, there would be a celebration at the school. There would be a dance and all these functions—cakewalks, musical chairs, fishpond. Fishpond was a game where you'd pay your money and they'd give you a stick with a string and a hook on it. You hang that over a sheet across the cloakroom door and they'd tie a prize on the hook.

The school was also the scene of carnivals held twice a year to raise money for their athletic equipment.

Friday was special for the Iona students. It was speech day. "We'd go into the one large room with a stage and every student—there were about forty-seven—would give an oral report of some kind. Sometimes they would give a speech, sometimes recite poetry or read aloud or give a book report," Watson says. And contrary to what you might think, absenteeism was not a problem on Fridays. "The peer pressure would get you up there if nothing else did," Watson adds.

The last hour of school on Fridays the students would again gather in the auditorium, this time to sing. "Mrs. Chappelle would come in to play the piano and we would sing and have a music lesson."

In those days, the school's newspaper contained items of interest to the parents as well as the students and carried notices of community meetings and public hearings as well as the covered dish suppers.

Charles Watson remembers the end of that era, too. By 1950–51, he was a student at Fort Myers High School and the Iona School was closed. The students and the principal were transferred to Fort Myers Beach.

William B. Mitchell, a flower grower, bought the old school building and used it to store glads until 1974, when Cole bought it for $75,000 and turned it into a design studio, later leasing it to Architectural Resources. Then, in October 1984, Condon bought the school and its site for $265,000, acquiring additional, adjacent acreage for another $80,000.

And, of course, the area has changed. Charles Watson says the Iona people were mostly farmers. The people from Punta Rassa whose children attended the school were commercial fishermen.

Today the farmers and fishermen are submerged beneath a sea of wealthy retirees and—more relevant to the Iona Schoolhouse—hordes of young businessmen who've brought their families to the milder climate of southwest Florida. This is the community the Iona Schoolhouse will serve now.

Originally published in the *Fort Myers News-Press*.

TICE ELEMENTARY
Second to None in the State
1927

I t is a far cry from the little log shanty in which Fort Myers children learned their three R's back in the early '70s to the seven modern school buildings in which the youth of today receive their education," wrote a *Tropical News* reporter in a special issue dated September 9, 1927. The '70s, of course, referred to the 1870s. The occasion was the opening of the school year, a year in which five new school buildings had been added. And the community was proud.

"When the 4,000 school children end their summer vacation and return to the 25 schools next Monday, they will find awaiting them a $2,000,000 school plant, second to none in the entire state of Florida," the reporter enthused.

Schools added were the new Tice School, Alva High School, Estero School, Olga School and a $25,000 addition to the school at Bonita Springs.

Tice was by far the most expensive. According to the *Fort Myers Daily Press*, the contract had been awarded in February to a local contractor, A.C. Rountree, for $133,300. Ede & Co. had snagged the contract for heating and plumbing at $8,713 and Thompson-Weatherly Electric had gotten the nod to do the electrical work for $1,989. In comparison, Alva cost $38,000; Estero, $30,000; Olga, $20,000.

The architect was William Sparklin, a somewhat obscure figure in that, according to Tice Elementary principal David Richards, he came to this area around 1925, left about 1930 and no one has heard from him since. According to the *Tropical News*, however, he also designed the schools at Olga and Alva.

Sparklin's work was apparently questioned, however, for the July 14 school board minutes included a rather cryptic comment. "In view of the adverse criticism of the Alva, Olga, and Tice school buildings," the minutes read, "it was voted that the written reports of all inspections and tests made by the architect shall be furnished the Board in order to correct any adverse impression and determine if it is necessary to receive other advice." It's interesting to note that in the September 9 issue, Sparklin is referred to as the architect in the news story describing Tice. However, in the caption beneath the photograph of the new school, Nat Gaillard Walker, the architect who designed the Federal Building, is listed as the architect of the Tice School.

Certainly the construction of Tice was very different. Even today, Richards describes the building as "massive," which it is. Richards says,

> *I have no way of proving it, but I just feel the architect had built the same school elsewhere. My reasoning is that it has a full basement which is unheard of for here because our water table is so high, it had rooms which would have been good for boilers which were never used because we used individual heaters and each entrance to the basement had an outside stairwell. When it rained, the water poured down those stairwells and flowed into the basement. In fact, since day one, surface water has been a problem at this school.*

In 1927, Tice was considered "one of the finest elementary schools in the state."

One building consisted of sixteen classrooms, three library rooms, principal's office, teachers' restrooms and an auditorium. There were three large rooms in the basement. Two were used as an indoor playground on rainy days. The other was proposed for a cafeteria. At the time, however, Richards says six of the eight classrooms on the first floor were used. The other two were adapted for the lunchroom. The actual cafeteria, in fact, was not built until 1955 and even today, Richards says the sink they use to wash dishes is still in the cloakroom.

One of the reasons Tice was both expensive and unusual was that it was fireproof. It was constructed of steel and cement. Richards says even the roof is of poured concrete. The floors were of a new material—mastic, a combination of rubber and asbestos. The stairs are iron.

The concern that the school be fireproof dated back to 1886, when Fort Myers's only school had burned. In fact, the subject was still so tender that the *Tropical News* reprinted a poem by local poet John C. Jeffcott originally published in 1886 that read in part, "Nor quarrel 'bout a school house fire…and all the bitterness 'twould make…About the rats that lit the match and did such damage with a scratch."

At the time, the burning of the school did arouse a great deal of bitterness. So much so that, as Karl Grismer writes in *The Story of Fort Myers*, this was actually the last straw that led to the separation of Lee from Monroe County. Commissioners at the county seat of Key West had responded to a delegation from Fort Myers requesting funds to build a new school that, Grismer writes, "since Fort Myers had been so careless as to permit a splendid $1,000 building to be destroyed by fire it didn't deserve" and there would be no money to build another school for at least a year. This also explains Fort Myers's determination to provide for its schools so that even though the school was technically in the county, Fort Myers provided water, sewer and gas.

At first, this arrangement was fine. But as people moved into Fort Myers and were hooked onto gas and water lines, the pressure dropped. Later the school was added to county utilities. And despite the fact that the school was considered fireproof, Richards says that the school was built with open flame hot-water radiators. These had no pilot lights and had to be manually lit.

The real story of Tice Elementary is contained in the faded, deteriorating records of the Tice PTA, carefully preserved by Tice's second principal Lora Belle Hays—a charge passed on and respected by Richards. These clippings and minutes tell of the school's tremendous involvement in the community. At the height of the Depression, for instance, the Tice PTA raised money to provide hot lunches and milk daily for nineteen children. The Christmas of 1931, they furnished sixteen families with toys and dolls. Parents' attendance was strongly encouraged and homeroom classes were given prizes for having the greatest number at a meeting. The minutes dutifully report that in May of 1933, Mrs. Osteen's third-grade class won and were given a party instead of a bowl of goldfish—because the goldfish were lost by accident.

The scrapbooks also trace inflation. For a PTA fish fry in 1933, they charged fifteen cents a plate and five cents for pie. By 1945, the price had soared to fifty cents a plate.

The 1930s were a period when everyone was concerned about John Barleycorn and Demon Rum. Mrs. W.P. Franklin, director of scientific temperance for the Woman's Christian Temperance Union (WCTU), was chairman of an essay contest. Young Tom Thurmond's essay entitled "Famous Abstainers" won glory for Tice School and netted him a year's subscription to *The Young Crusader*, a temperance magazine.

Over the years, Tice Elementary School has continued to play an important and stable role in its community. There have been only four principals: Mrs. Frank L. Ross, from 1927 to 1930; Lora Belle Hayes, from 1930 to 1961; David Richards, from 1961 to 1964; and Fred Hudson, from 1964 to 1967. Richards returned in 1967 and has been there since.

The school's doors are still open to its residents. It's been a shelter to its people during hurricanes; the last one, of course, was Donna. Neighborhood children still march down its halls and study in its classrooms. In the evening, congregate meals are served to senior citizens and community and adult education classes are offered. Its grounds are busy on weekends for it is now the site of a county park with picnic tables, lighted tennis courts and an unlighted baseball field for practice.

The county is building a swimming pool, which is another indicator of inflation—Richards says the pool will cost in the neighborhood of $300,000. And the renovation project now in the works will further secure Tice Elementary's future. The Lee County School Board has selected the architectural firm of Rivers & Pigott to oversee the renovation. Eugene Pigott is an alumnus of Tice so he'll have a special interest in preserving a part of his heritage. Architect Bill Rivers, who's been here since 1941, says the plan is to return the exterior to the look of the 1920s while upgrading the interior to the 1980s.

With luck, they'll be able to remove the spraycrete from the medallions adorning the school building and maybe even from the cast stone face of the horned man who spews a fountain of water at the front of the school.

Next time you drive by the Tice Elementary School on Tice Street in east Fort Myers, slow down. Take a moment to appreciate this lovely old building that's still playing an important role in its neighborhood.

Originally published in "Only Yesterday" in the *Fort Myers News-Press* in 1985.

Tamiami
Trailblazing
1928

Today drivers avoid the Tamiami Trail (U.S. 41) saying it's crowded, clogged and dangerous. However, when first opened in April of 1928, it was widely hailed as the engineering marvel of the twentieth century, even dubbed the Appian Way of the USA.

Furthermore, the Tamiami Trail answered a burning question. Thomas Alva Edison said, "There is only one Fort Myers and 90 million people are going to find it out." The question for many years was, how?

Until the construction of the Tamiami Trail, Fort Myers was accessible only by boat, train and wagon. Because of the lack of roads, you could hardly get here from Miami. And traveling here from Tampa was equally as difficult.

But the opening of the Tamiami Trail changed that, admitting the rest of the world to a swamp peopled by Seminoles and a remote cow territory previously a playground for wealthy sportsmen. The editor of the *Fort Myers Press* labeled the opening of the Tamiami Trail on April 25, 1928, as "the greatest day in the history of the State of Florida."

Dr. Fons Hathaway, then chairman of the Florida Highway Commission, likened the trail to the Appian Way, commenting that Appius Claudius, the builder of the famous Roman highway, encountered similar obstacles twenty-two centuries earlier, including crossing a treacherous swamp.

Assumapatchee was one of the Seminole guides who led the Tamiami Trailblazers through the Everglades. This photo is proof of the magnitude of their accomplishment, for the Everglades was truly a jungle. *Courtesy of the Southwest Florida Historical Museum.*

And people who've chafed impatiently during completion of I-75 in recent years have nothing on the earlier residents of our area, for construction of the trail was a stop-and-go proposition.

In the 1939 Federal Writers Project *Florida: A Guide to the Southernmost State*, Captain J.F. Jaudon of Ochopee is credited with having conceived the idea of the Tamiami Trail in 1914. Jaudon was president of the Chevelier Corporation, which owned vast tracts of land in northern Monroe County. (The name—Tamiami Trail, coined by combining Tampa and Miami—was

105

dreamed up by L.P. Dickie of Tampa while at a meeting of the Good Roads Boosters in Orlando in 1917.)

Construction began in 1915, financed by communities establishing themselves as road and bridge districts with authority to issue bonds. However, progress was delayed because communities were unable to accurately project the amount of money needed and soon ran short of funds. Additionally, America's entry into World War I resulted in a manpower shortage.

However, Dade County voters coughed up $275,000 and completed its section of the trail in 1918. The first local link was a nine-foot-wide, hard-surface road between Fort Myers and Naples, plus a side road to Marco. A $177,500 bond issue provided for that.

The same year, voters in Everglades City approved a bond issue to raise $125,000 for their section. A concrete bridge, finished in 1921, spanned Charlotte Harbor and connected Punta Gorda to Tampa.

Progress slammed to a halt when the contractor reached the Lee County line. (At this time, Lee included Collier County as well.) To get things moving, trail supporters in Fort Myers—led by Captain E.E. Damkohler—ferried their cars across the Caloosahatchee and then took the wagon trail to Punta Gorda. Other motorists joined them and they proceeded on to Tampa. As a result, a $74,000 bond issue passed to build a road from the Caloosahatchee to the Charlotte County line. Charlotte voters approved a $150,000 bond issue to construct their section. Work began in 1922.

Next trail boosters formed a company in Fort Myers to construct a wooden bridge across the Caloosahatchee. They planned to collect tolls. However, construction was about three-fourths completed when the State Road Department determined they couldn't do that. As a result, the County took over the project.

Now it was 1923 and progress had again slowed, for many people felt it was impossible to build a road across the Everglades. In fact, according to Charlton Tebeau, writing *A History of Florida*, the state legislature created Collier County in 1923 largely because of Barron Collier's promise (he owned three-fourths of the land there) that he would push construction of the trail.

And Jaudon was not about to surrender. He journeyed to Fort Myers and hassled the Board of Trade (forerunner of today's Chamber of Commerce) about the highway. There, he joined forces with local businessman Ora Chapin, another ardent supporter of the trail. The duo hatched a plan to revive public interest: they would prove automobiles could cross the Everglades by doing it. Chapin set out to find men willing to brave the rigors of the swamp.

By late March 1923, he'd rounded up twenty-three volunteers from Tampa, Sarasota, Estero and Fort Myers. Joined by two Seminole Indian guides, Little Billie Cornapatchee and Abraham Lincoln (Assumapatchee was his Indian name), the group now known as the Trailblazers began the trek on April 4. They were traveling in eight Ford Model Ts, an Elcar and an Overland. They estimated the journey would take three days and they had food for three days. (It took twenty-three.)

Even Thomas Edison was on hand. He gave one of the Trailblazers a bottle of grape juice with instructions to deliver it to his friend William Jennings Bryan, who was selling real estate in Coral Gables.

The first day's journey over graded roads was a cinch, but the next morning they ran into trouble. The Elcar, a heavy car, immediately bogged down in the muck and had to turn back. The Overland's front wheelbase was cracked. One of the Model Ts was disabled when the universal was twisted so that by the end of the second day, the caravan was reduced to seven Fords.

Sending scouts ahead to determine their path, for there were no maps, the group decided their next stop should be Everglades City. They spent the night as Barron G. Collier's guests at his hotel. The next morning, armed with additional food and supplies, the Trailblazers pushed off on the next lap.

Once past the Fakahatchee Strand, they used machetes to slash their way through sawgrass so high they couldn't see the car ahead of them. They slogged through miles of open marsh and cypress stands. The younger men worked their way ahead of the cars, cutting down trees to clear a path. Because the ground was so wet, the lead cars left deep ruts. In order to keep the Fords from getting stuck, the men ripped bromeliads and wild orchids from the trees and used them to fill the ruts.

Before long, supplies were exhausted. They even drank the grape juice. The Indian guides were sent to find food. Abe Lincoln returned with a deer, but Little Billie Cornapatchee lost his way and turned back. They knew they'd been reported as lost because a search plane had flown overhead. And although they yelled and waved, they were obscured from view by the swamp and were not seen. They struggled on.

The odometer on one of the Model Ts indicated they'd traveled one hundred miles. One of the advance scouts returned to report they'd found a survey stake, which meant they were on Chevelier land in north Monroe County. By noon of that day, they'd met three men from the survey party who'd heard they were lost. The Trailblazers replenished their gas tanks and headed to the surveyors' camp, anticipating their first decent meal in days.

It took them hours to travel the twelve miles to camp and the last couple feet were muck and every car got stuck. Using poles, they literally pried the first two cars from the muck, slipping branches into the ruts to keep the cars from bogging down again. The surveyors had almost completed their work in the area so supplies were limited. But they shared what they had: canned corned beef, canned tomatoes and a loaf of bread.

The following morning as the Trailblazers were extricating the five remaining Fords from the muck, a plane landed and unloaded fresh supplies sent by the Miami Chamber of Commerce.

Now they were sure the worst was over and that evening as they rested around a campfire, they sang the words to the song they'd written (the melody was "Tipperary") to commemorate the event:

> *It's a long way to old Miami*
> *It's a long way to go*
> *It's a long way to old Miami*
> *Over a trail we did not know.*
> *Goodbye old Fort Myers*
> *Estero and Naples, too*
> *It's a long, long way to Miami*
> *But we went right through.*

After a journey of two weeks, they were now five miles from Miami.

And it would take them another full week to cover that last stretch.

They had planned to start on the last lap of their trip the following morning, but it rained. For three straight days, the rain poured down.

In the meantime, the plight of the Trailblazers had made the front pages of nearly every major newspaper in the country. The men were thought to be dead, the victims of alligators, bears or cottonmouth moccasins.

Now, however, as they emerged from the swamp after a journey lasting an incredible twenty-three days, they learned they were national heroes. Newspaper reporters and cameramen dogged their steps, demanding interviews. In one instance, they were taken back into the woods and asked to demonstrate for the media how they'd dug their cars out of the mud.

By the time they straggled into Miami and the flashbulbs had dimmed and the frenetic reporters were off chasing other stories, they had accomplished far more than they had dreamed possible. Of course, they'd proved cars could make the trip through the Everglades. Even more important, their exploits focused so much national attention on the Tamiami Trail that interest revived and construction soon began again.

The hard part was still ahead—construction of a road across the Everglades. A *Fort Myers Press* reporter wrote, "Giant dredges have splashed and ploughed their way over miles to throw up the rock base in the very heart of the jungle where men worked in water waist deep…30 sticks of dynamite were exploded each five feet over almost the entire route to break the surface of the limerock." Construction of the two-lane, 275-mile Tamiami Trail cost between $7 and $9 million. The *Tropical News* reported the men building the trail used 2,598,000 sticks of dynamite. An average of 150 men working on the road completed only 1¼ miles a month. The final 45½ miles took nearly four years.

The events marking the opening of the Tamiami Trail almost exactly five years later celebrated far more than a road—they celebrated the courage and persistence of the road crews and the ingenious intelligence of the engineers and builders who figured out how to accomplish the seemingly impossible.

And what a celebration! The Fort Myers City Commission allocated $1,000 to fund local ceremonies. Local realtor Henry Colquitt was quoted in the *Press* as predicting that five hundred cars would be crossing Florida on the trail.

"If half that number were to stop in Fort Myers," Colquitt fretted, "we would find ourselves at a loss to take care of them." Later, as the date grew nearer, the *Press* reported five thousand people were expected in Fort Myers and asked citizens "to throw open their homes," which they did.

Wednesday, April 25, at 8:30 a.m., the motorcade left Tampa headed for Miami via the Tamiami Trail, arriving here late that afternoon. Earlier a procession including County Commission Chairman John E. Morris, Fort Myers Mayor Elmer Hough, Barron Collier and Dr. Hathaway had headed north to the Charlotte County line. There they joined the pioneering motorists from Tampa and made a triumphant entrance.

While they were en route, attention was temporarily diverted to a "daring stunt pilot from Tampa" who married his sweetheart in an airplane high in the cloudy skies between Tampa and Fort Myers.

In the meantime, a temporary stadium had been erected in the city park here and a three-hour program that evening included recognition of the mayors of Palmetto, Tampa and Ocala and the secretary of the Orange County Commission. Special music was provided and a street dance followed the formalities. The 116th Field Artillery even sponsored a special fight card.

The highlight, however, had to be the "first public address ever made by a Seminole Indian to white men." According to the *Press*, Abraham Lincoln, one of the Trailblazers' guides, "welcomed the gas buggies of his white brothers into the Everglades."

The next morning, motorists left at 5:00 a.m. so they'd have time to take in the sights at the Everglades, where Collier County was hosting its first fair.

The celebration climaxed with ceremonies the next day when 390 cars, including nearly 100 from Fort Myers, arrived in Miami.

Today we avoid the Tamiami Trail, but it served us well for decades. And somehow, the opening of I-75—although also an "engineering marvel"—pales in comparison. No bands have paraded. No politicians have mesmerized audiences with their eloquence. Instead, cars spilled, without ceremony, onto the gray lanes of asphalt as access roads have opened.

Originally published in "Only Yesterday" in the *Fort Myers News-Press* on April 18, 1984.

CAPE CORAL
Water Wonderland
1957

On the eighteenth of August this year, 1990, the city of Cape Coral, originally pitched as a Water Wonderland because of its 400-plus miles of manmade canals, officially lost its teenage status and lurched into its second decade. A lot has happened during those years. The patch of property known during the Seminole Wars as the site of the Harney Point Massacre and later as a cattle range is today a bustling 115-square-mile community with a population of 70,000 vocal and vociferous residents—a young community flexing its muscles in the governmental scheme of things, saying, listen to me, I'm important, too.

Cape Coral today is a city with problems, but those problems are endemic to growth—the need for a larger sewer system, better roads and water. But it's also a city with potential. Rapid growth has brought an ever-increasing tax base, both in terms of individuals and businesses, an increasingly younger population and a sense of civic pride and involvement unmatched elsewhere in Lee County.

To be precise, this date is actually the twentieth anniversary of Cape Coral's incorporation as a city. Cape Coral was really born in 1957 in the minds of Leonard and Jack Rosen of Baltimore, Maryland. The Rosens were multimillionaires who'd made their fortune via Charles Antell cosmetics. According to Eileen Bernard, writing in her history of Cape Coral titled

The entrance to Cape Coral when it opened in 1957. *Photo from the author's collection.*

Lies That Came True, Leonard Rosen's brainstorm was to merchandise land the same way he'd merchandised the cosmetics.

By November of 1957, the Rosens closed on the $678,000 purchase of the 103-square-mile parcel of land from Granville Keller and Franklin Miles and the Rosens formed their company: Gulf American Land Corp.

Across the river, old-timers in Fort Myers were laughing up their shirtsleeves at the two city slickers. Why shoot, that land wasn't good for

In 1966, Cape Coral developers Leonard (left) and Jack Rosen introduced comedian Bob Hope, who appeared at the dedication to the AMVETS of a carillon in the Rose Garden. *Courtesy of Eileen Bernard.*

nothin' but a little huntin' and pasturin' cows. But the old-timers hadn't figured on the Rosens' marketing scheme—the brothers from Baltimore weren't going to sell to locals who knew better, they were going to sell to other city slickers who *didn't* know better.

And it worked. The Rosens flew them in from New York City, from Chicago, from Newark, from Detroit. Wined and dined the sheep—er, prospects—and kept them too busy to figure out what they were hearing and seeing, too busy to think straight. Herded them into tight planes and buses for tours of barren wilderness that would—in their lifetimes, honest!—be transformed into a metropolis. Kept them penned up in closing rooms for endless hours until they signed on the dotted line and emerged as befuddled, bedazzled owners of a piece of the dream.

And the dream worked.

Of course, there were some tough times. In June of 1967, the *Wall Street Journal* ran an article accusing Gulf American of a laundry list of illegal practices including lot switching, revising plat plans without approval, using high-pressure and deceptive sales techniques and using misleading sales materials.

But the dream worked.

And Cape Coral survived and prospered as a city through the lean years, legal travails and even the eventual bankruptcy of its parent company, Gulf American.

By 1970, the Waterfront Wonderland with its four hundred miles of manmade canals had a population of 11,470. Agreeing for once in the community's history, the population voted to incorporate, did so and in December elected Paul Fickinger its first mayor. In short order, a police department was staffed and in place, a city hall was constructed and the City of Cape Coral was in full swing. With a government structure in place, the pace of progress was accelerated.

The 1970s Were Hectic

A major problem was that the fledgling city found itself striving to provide services for a population that nearly tripled within the decade. By 1980, the residents numbered more than 32,000; however, the most significant change in Cape Coral would not occur until the 1980s, when it completed its transformation from a bedroom community to a full-blown municipality.

"When I started practicing law here in 1968," says state Senator Fred Dudley, "I was the second full-time attorney. I think the biggest change is that now you can do your shopping here where in the past you had to go to Fort Myers. The business community out here, most of them being fairly small businesses, has grown. Now we have thirty attorneys, our own hospital, and our own high school. You can even buy a car here now. We have one Chevrolet dealership and I'm sure we'll have others along SR 78 [Pine Island Road] as it gets four-laned in the next few years."

Neither the expansion of Cape Coral's business community nor its transformation are accidental. According to Mayor Joe Mazurkiewicz, who's in the middle of his fourth term, "Since the early 1980s, we have made a conscious drive to attract commercial and industrial growth for the fiscal benefits as well as providing the necessary retail and service establishments to eliminate the need to travel back and forth across the river so much. It was a fiscal reality that if we stayed as a bedroom community our taxes would have gone up so high that without a commercial and industrial tax base, we just couldn't afford to live here."

Asked to describe Cape Coral today, Dudley says, "It's a great place to live and raise a family." Mazurkiewicz says, "It's an emerging metropolitan area just starting to grab hold of commercial, industrial and economic bases...for the first time, a very well-planned community with a state comprehensive growth management plan is in place."

Both Dudley and Mazurkiewicz have lived in Cape Coral for a considerable length of time. Both men have businesses in town—Dudley, his law practice; Mazurkiewicz, an electrical contracting firm. Both men have a strong sense of civic pride and community loyalty. On the other hand, Steve Otte has only been around for a year and a half. However, he's the editor of *The Breeze*—Cape Coral's newspaper—and sees Cape Coral from a different perspective.

His description of Cape Coral is that of a town so politically divided it impedes its own progress. "Cape Coral people have a predilection for political infighting. As soon as one issue seems settled, they find something else to fight over...hardly anything gets done in the city because the factions are perfectly balanced on the council. Anything controversial that's brought up by one faction is blocked by the other side and vice versa."

Cape writer and historian Eileen Bernard agrees that the residents of Cape Coral are confrontational and adds, "I think there are more restrictive rules and government regulations than in the first twelve years [prior to incorporation]. In the old days, it was a very unstructured place and nobody knew or cared much what the rules were."

Restrictive rules are certainly best exemplified by reference to the truck parking ordinance, which prohibits residents from parking even their pickup trucks in their driveways. And it is without doubt that Cape Coral has a reputation for being a community of shoutin', scrappin' folks who will argue about anything, any time and any place, although their favorite arena is Cape Coral City Hall.

Dudley praises that spirit. "Cape Coral is a real melting pot, much more so than the city of Fort Myers, for example. Most people here came from someplace else. A lot of these people come from areas where they attended town hall meetings once or twice a month. They're used to having some input into how their city is run. And they tend to be a lot more participatory when they come to Cape Coral. In our elections, we have high voter turnouts. You'll find a number of contested races for city council, much more than you will in a more established community."

WHAT'S AHEAD IN 2000?

If Cape Coral has changed so dramatically in the past two decades, what will the city be like in the year 2000? The first adjective that comes to mind is *big*. Projections call for the population to double from the current 70,000 to 140,000. As for the other challenges incumbent in such growth, the city's comprehensive growth management plan contains provisions for water, sewers, conservation, funding sources, parks and roads.

Dudley and Mazurkiewicz agree on two transportation projects that will have a vital impact on the quality of that growth. The first is the four-laning of SR 78 "to a commercial corridor." That, Mazurkiewicz says, "will provide retail sales establishments and also an industrial job base." The second is the construction of the hotly contested midpoint bridge. "The midpoint bridge being done would connect to the east/west corridor and then to Burnt Store Road, which would provide a major transportation link to I-75 and North Port Charlotte to Burnt Store Road," he says And certainly, however it's done, moving 140,000 people is going to be a major challenge that must be faced in the very near future.

Cape Coral in the year 2000 as envisioned by Eileen Bernard—and she readily admits it's an idealistic vision—will find

> *people living together in the shade of a thousand trees, people enjoying peace and prosperity as a result of having dealt well with problems such as growth, increased sensitivity to the environment, and having taken advantage of the great technological changes that I think are coming...strong but sensible rules and regulations enacted and enforced by an enlightened government and a well-informed community working together instead of in a state of continual confrontation.*

In her book, Bernard, who worked for Gulf American Land at the time, writes that "Leonard Rosen stood on a big mound of earth, waving his arms like Moses on the mount, and proclaimed to his chief engineer, 'There will be a great city here some day,' then added with a laugh, 'in spite of us.'"

Perhaps it's time to add another epithet to Rosen's job description—business magnate, cosmetics mogul, land developer, speculator, male chauvinist, philanthropist and finally, prophet.

Update: The U.S. Census for the year 2000 reported there were 109,286 people, 40,768 households and 30,209 families residing in the city. Four years later, according to the U.S. Census Bureau's 2004 estimates, the city had grown to 127,985, making it the largest city in southwest Florida.

Originally published in the November–December 1990 issue of *Lee Living*.

SANIBEL
"We Call It Paradise"
1974

In Sanibel's halcyon days BC (Before Causeway), the island was unquestionably an unspoiled tropical paradise. The pace was slow. The residents were friendly. Everyone knew everyone else. As late as 1962, Lee Countians would take the ferry and loll the day away shelling, picnicking and strolling the beach. They didn't go often because they had to stay the entire day; Kinzie's ferry came only twice daily. As the sun careened below the horizon, they would board the ferry sunburned and tired, but at peace. There was no traffic on the island and nothing to do but relax and enjoy. Furthermore, they were not labeled "daytrippers."

Then on May 26, 1963, the ferry—which had been operating since 1926—made its symbolic last voyage as politicians scissored the ribbon on the Sanibel Causeway overhead. Sanibel was now easily, if expensively, accessible to the rest of the world.

However, to be fair, many of the attributes that made Sanibel so attractive in the 1800s remain. Sanibel historian Elinor Dormer in 1990 said, "We love the natural environment, the birds, the beach, the shells, the nature trails, our own home and neighborhood which hasn't changed too much." Adds Ken Meeker, executive director of the Chamber of Commerce, "First on the list of Sanibel's assets are the beaches and the shells. Second is that nearly half of the island is a nature preserve. Third

For years Sanibel was noted not only for its pristine beauty, but also for the splendid shelling to be found on its beaches. *Photo from the author's collection.*

is the ambiance; nothing is over three stories. Fourth, it's just a nice place. We call it paradise."

But changes began almost before that first car drove across the causeway. As early as 1967, it became obvious to the residents of Sanibel that something had to be done to limit development and protect the environment. Triggering their concern was a report filed by a planning firm hired by Lee County Commissioners. The out-of-town consultants recommended a four-lane highway be constructed through Ding Darling Sanctuary and high rises be permitted in other sections of Sanibel.

The solution became as obvious as the problem and in 1974, Sanibel residents voted to incorporate. The Florida legislature granted the charter and in December of that year, Sanibel's first five-member council took office: Porter Goss, Vernon MacKenzie, Charles LeBuff, Zelda Butler and Francis Bailey.

An interesting side note to Sanibel's history was documented by Dormer, whose research revealed that this was the second time Sanibel had been incorporated. In her excellently written book entitled *The Seashell Islands,* she mentions the original incorporation of Sanibel, which occurred in 1832, and adds that by 1844, "no one remained in the island settlements for the U.S. military had deemed it unwise to leave anyone there possibly to trade with the Indians."

Still another intriguing aspect to the island's history is that although it became popular as a resort in the 1890s, it was also noted for its citrus groves and truck farms. By 1896, farmers were shipping a thousand crates of tomatoes a week during the growing season. A few years later, crops included eggplant, beets, squash, green peppers, cucumbers and beans. The torrential tides of salt water accompanying the 1921 hurricane destroyed the groves and arid farms and marked finis to Sanibel's agricultural industry.

Since that time, Sanibel's economic base has been and still is largely founded on tourism. Today the island is a world-renowned resort area, a fact that has created its own set of problems. With the accessibility provided by the Sanibel Causeway, tourism has grown to the point that the tiny island's roads are as clogged during tourist season as cholesterol-laden arteries. And "high season" lasts from Christmas to Easter, a good third of the year.

If there are vehicles, it follows that there must be people and indeed Sanibel's population of approximately 5,500 year-round residents swells to better than 15,000 in the winter and that figure includes only winter residents, not vacationers. That's a lot of folks on an island roughly twenty-two square miles in an area that stretches about fifteen miles from tip to tip and is two miles at its widest point.

Moreover, vacationers are so taken with the island's beauty that they often decide to move there. As a result, the population has nearly doubled, surging from 2,875 full-time residents in 1975. That growth has created additional problems. More people means more demands on the water supply, on roads, on the police and fire departments. A heightened market for a finite land supply inevitably results in higher prices for that land and, hence, higher taxes. If traffic and tourists are two burrs in Sanibel's triple crown of thorns, then undoubtedly high property taxes are the third.

Average per capita income is high—$52,463—but taxes are still formidable. Dormer, who has lived on Sanibel year-round since 1962, says, "A lot of people we would like to stay here, good citizens, contributing residents, have to sell out because they can't afford to pay that much money to live here. It's getting out of sight: Our taxes are $9,000 this year."

High taxes are definitely having an impact. Drive up and down the streets on Sanibel and you'll see a plethora of for sale signs posted on the neatly kept lawns.

Dormer also points to pioneers like the Woodring family, whose ancestors settled on the island in 1888. Today they must pay exorbitant taxes because so many million-dollar homes have been built around them. "When there's anything like that," Dormer explains, "the taxes are based on what you could get if you sell your home. They don't consider, and never have, that you might just want to live there."

And this leads to still another change—in attitude. New residents are apparently unaware that Sanibel was settled by pioneer families whose members worked as farmers and commercial fishermen. Being moneyed—as you must today to be able to afford living there—and status conscious, these newcomers have adopted a possessive and somewhat superior attitude. They are not known for welcoming those they label derisively as "daytrippers." Dormer is outspoken about the attitude.

"Except for the old-timers, I think Sanibel people tend to look at daytrippers with contempt! I tell them, 'For heavens sakes, you're daytrippers when you go on vacation.' I don't like that attitude, but yes, it does exist."

And that attitude has created—at least in the old-timers' camp—a rift. But a change in attitude was inevitable.

Sanibel is no longer a pristine wilderness retreat where locals go to escape the pressures of day-to-day life on the mainland. Even off-season, Sanibel teems with expensive restaurants and boutiques.

What's ahead for the island paradise? When pressed, Acting City Manager Bill Mills offers two scenarios for the year 2000. "My worst scenario," opines Mills, "would be heavy wall-to-wall development along the lines of Florida's east coast and that Sanibel loses the appeal it has being an environmentally conscious community that makes everyone want to come here."

And the best? Mills replies, "That we continue to proceed with the development of the island within the Comprehensive Land Use Plan and when we do reach this mystical, magical build out of the island—that is, our complete density as assigned in the plan—that we are able to maintain it. And, if indeed we get involved in lawsuits, that the courts agree this is all the development the island can maintain."

Update: By 2001, according to the City of Sanibel's official website, Sanibel's year-round population was 6,072 and seasonal population was 33,000. In that same year, 3,152,058 vehicles crossed the Sanibel Causeway.

Originally published in the fall 1990 issue of *Lee Living*.

BIBLIOGRAPHY

Akerman, Joe A., Jr. *Florida Cowman: A History of Florida Cattle Raising*. Perry, FL: Jimbob Printing Inc., 1989.

Andrews, Allen H. *A Yank Pioneer in Florida*. Jacksonville: Douglas Printing Co., 1950.

Beater, Jack. *Pirates and Buried Treasure*. St. Petersburg: Great Outdoors, 1959.

———. *Tales of South Florida and the 10,000 Islands*. St. Petersburg: Great Outdoors, 1950.

Bernard, Eileen. *Lies That Came True*. Ocoee, FL: Anna Publishing, 1983.

Dacy, George F. *Four Centuries of Florida Ranching*. Privately printed. St. Louis, MO: Britt Printing Co., 1940.

Dormer, Elinor. *The Seashell Islands*. Tallahassee: Rose Printing Co., 1979.

Federal Writers Project. *Florida: A Guide to the Southernmost State*. 1939.

BIBLIOGRAPHY

Fritz, Florence. *Unknown Florida*. Privately published.

————. *The Unknown Story of World Famous Sanibel and Captiva*. Privately published.

Grismer, Karl. *The Story of Fort Myers*. St. Petersburg: St. Petersburg Printing Co., 1949.

Hanna, A.J., and Kathryn Abbey. *Lake Okeechobee: Wellspring of the Everglades*. Indianapolis: Bobbs-Merrill, 1948.

Kerr, John Law. *The Legend of Useppa*. Privately published, 1940.

Pearse, Eleanor H.D. *Florida's Vanishing Era: From the Journals of a Young Girl and her Father, 1887 to 1910*. Privately published, 1949.

Remington, Frederic. *Crooked Trails*. New York: Harper & Brothers, 1898.

Stonestreet, Don. *The History of the Fort Myers Fire Department*. Dallas: Taylor Publishing, 1993.

Tebeau, Charlton W. *A History of Florida*. Miami: University of Miami Press, 1971.

ABOUT THE AUTHOR

Remembering Lee County is Prudy Taylor Board's sixteenth published book and is a companion book to *Remembering Fort Myers: The City of Palms*, published in 2006 by The History Press.

As a freelance journalist, Prudy had more than a thousand articles published in regional and national magazines. She was a staff writer for the *Fort Myers News-Press*, assignment editor and reporter for WINK-TV (CBS) and WBBH-TV (NBC) and managing editor of two regional magazines: *Lee Living* and *Home & Condo*. She is now a freelance writer and project editor with Taylor & Francis, an international publisher of general interest nonfiction and technical and medical books.

Prudy's first book, *Lee County: A Pictorial History*, was published in 1985. Other books include *One Man's Vision: The History of the Port Royal Club in Naples, Florida; Pages From The Past; Historic Fort Myers, Florida; Venice, Florida, Through the Years; The Belleview Biltmore Hotel: A Century of Hospitality; The Renaissance Vinoy: St. Petersburg's Crown Jewel; Mending Minds, Healing Hearts: The History of the Florida Sheriffs Youth Ranches; The History of Barry University; The History of Dania Beach, FL: 100 Years of Pioneer Spirit* and *The History of the Dunes Beach and Golf Club*. Her fiction includes *Murder a la Carte, Blood Legacy* and *The Vow*.

Visit us at
www.historypress.net